Justin Huntly McCarthy

An Outline of Irish History, from the Earliest Times to the Present Day

Justin Huntly McCarthy

An Outline of Irish History, from the Earliest Times to the Present Day

ISBN/EAN: 9783744741088

Printed in Europe, USA, Canada, Australia, Japan

Cover: Foto ©ninafisch / pixelio.de

More available books at **www.hansebooks.com**

OF

IRISH HISTORY

*FROM THE EARLIEST TIMES TO THE
PRESENT DAY.*

BY

JUSTIN H. McCARTHY

BALTIMORE
JOHN MURPHY & CO.
1883

CONTENTS.

CHAPTER	PAGE
I. THE LEGENDS	7
II. CHRISTIANITY	21
III. THE NORMAN CONQUEST	27
IV. ELIZABETH	39
V. THE CROMWELLIAN SETTLEMENT	49
VI. THE RESTORATION—WILLIAM OF ORANGE	59
VII. THE EIGHTEENTH CENTURY	67
VIII. EMMET—O'CONNELL	83
IX. YOUNG IRELAND—FENIANISM	95
X. THE LAND QUESTION	106
XI. HOME RULE—THE LAND LEAGUE	116

AN OUTLINE OF IRISH HISTORY.

CHAPTER I.

THE LEGENDS.

As we peer doubtfully into the dim past of Irish history we seem to stand like Odysseus at the yawning mouth of Hades. The thin shades troop about us, and flit hither and thither fitfully in shadowy confusion. Stately kings sweep by in their painted chariots. Yellow-haired heroes rush to battle shaking their spears and shouting their war-songs, while the thick gold torques rattle on arm and throat, and their many-coloured cloaks stream on the wind. They sweep by and are lost to sight, and their places are taken by others in a shifting, splendid, confused pageant of monarchs and warriors, and beautiful women for whose love the heroes are glad to die and the kings to peril their crowns; and amongst them all move the majestic white-robed bards, striking their golden harps and telling the tales of the days of old, and handing down the names of heroes for ever. What may we hope to distinguish of this weltering world of regal figures, whirled by before our eyes as on that infernal wind which seared the eyes of Dante? The traveller in Egypt goes down into the Tombs of the Kings at ancient Thebes. By the flaring flicker of a candle he discerns dimly on the walls about him endless processions of painted figures—the images of kings and beggars, of soldiers and slaves, of the teeming life of ages—portrayed in glowing colours all around. It is but for a moment, while his candle is slowly burning down, that he seems to stand in the thronged centuries of Egyptian dynasties with all their named and nameless figures; and then he passes out again into the upper air and level sunlight of the Theban valley, as one who has dreamed a chaotic dream.

Groping in the forgotten yesterday of Irish legend is like this groping in an Egyptian tomb. We are in a great sepulchral chamber—a hall of the dead, whose walls are pictured with endless figures, huddled together in bewildering fantastic medley. What can we make out, holding up our thin taper and gazing doubtfully at the storied walls? Yon fair woman, with the crowd of girls about her, is the Lady Ceasair, who came to Ireland before the deluge with fifty women and three men, Bith, Ladra, and Fintain. The waters swept away this curiously proportioned colony, and their place was taken 'in the sixtieth year of the age of Abraham' by the parricide Partholan, of the stock of Japhet. For three hundred years his descendants ruled, until a pestilence destroyed them all. The Nemedhians, under Nemedh, loomed up from the shores of the Black Sea and swarmed over Ireland. They were harassed by plagues and by incessant battlings with the Fomorians, a race of savage sea-kings, descendants of Cham, who had settled in the Western Isles. In the end the Fomorians triumphed; they drove out the remnant of Nemedhians whom plague and sword had spared. This remnant fled, some to the north of Europe to become the ancestors of the Firbolgs, some to Greece to give a parentage to the Tuatha de Danann, and some to Britain, which took its name from the Nemedhian leader, Briotan-Maol.

After a time, the first of the Nemedhian refugees, the Firbolgs, came back to Ireland, to be soon dispossessed by another invasion of Nemedhian descendants, the Tuatha de Danann, who came from Greece, and who were deeply skilled in all wizardries. Their sorceries stood them in good stead, for the Firbolgs made a fierce resistance. A desperate battle was fought, in which the Firbolg king was slain. His grave is still shown on the Sligo strand, and it is fabled that the tide will never cover it. Nuada, the king of the Tuatha de Danann, lost his right hand in this fight, and seems to have gone near losing his kingship in consequence, as his warlike people would have refused to recognize a mutilated monarch. But there were cunning artificers among the Greeks. One of these fashioned a silver hand for the king, who was known as Nuada of the Silver Hand ever after. The first of ' The Three Sorrowful Tales of Erin ' belongs to the reign of this Sovereign with the Argent Fist—the tale of the fate of the children of Turenn. The three sons of Turenn, Brian, Ur, and Urcar, killed Kian father of Luga of the Long Arms, and one of the three sons of Canta, with whom the three sons of Turenn were at feud. Six times the sons of Turenn buried the body of their victim, and six times the earth cast it up again, but on the seventh burial the body remained in the grave. As the sons of Turenn rode from the spot a faint voice came from the ground, warning them that the blood they had spilled would follow them to the fulfilment of their doom. Luga of the Long Arms, seeking for his father, came to the grave, and there the stones of the earth took voice and told him that his father lay beneath. Luga unearthed the body, and vowed vengeance on the sons of Turenn over it. He then hastened to Tara, to the court of Nuada of the Silver Hand, and denounced the sons of Turenn. In those days the friends of any murdered person might either receive a fine, called ' eric,' in compensation, or might seek the death of the murderer. Luga called for the ' eric.' He demanded three apples, the skin of a pig, a spear, two steeds and a chariot, seven pigs, a hound-whelp, a cooking-spit, and three shouts on a hill. To this ' eric ' the sons of Turenn agreed readily enough before all the court. Then Luga explained himself more fully. The three apples were to be plucked from the garden of Hisberna, in the east of the world. They were the colour of burnished gold, and of the taste of honey, and cured wounds and all manner of sickness, and had many other wonderful qualities. The garden of Hisberna was carefully guarded, and none were allowed to take its precious fruit. The pig-skin belonged to the King of Greece, and possessed the power of healing whosoever touched it. The spear was a venomed weapon with a blazing head, belonging to the King of Persia. The two steeds and chariot belonged to the King of Sicily. The seven pigs were the delight of Asal, King of the Golden Pillars, for they could be killed and eaten one day, and become alive and well the next. The hound-whelp belonged to the King of Iroda, and every wild beast of the forest fell powerless before it. The cooking-spit belonged to the warlike women of the Island of Fincara, who never yet gave a cooking-spit to anyone who did not overcome them in battle. The hill on which the three shouts had to be given was the hill of Midkena, in the north of Lochlann, the country of the Danes, which was always guarded by Midkena and his sons, who never allowed anyone to shout on it.

The sons of Turenn were much daunted by this terrible 'eric,' but they were bound to fulfil it. They set sail in an enchanted canoe, the *Wave Sweeper*, to the garden of Hisberna, and succeeded, by turning themselves into hawks, in carrying off the apples. They then visited Greece in the guise of learned poets from Erin, and after a desperate fight overcame the King of Greece and his champions, and carried off the pig-skin. Leaving the shores of Greece 'and all its blue streams,' they sailed to Persia, where they had to fight another battle with the king before they could carry off the blazing weapon in triumph. They then voyaged to Sicily, overcame its monarch, and drove off the famous chariot and horses. Next came the turn of Asal, King of the Golden Pillars, but their fame had gone before them, and Asal gave up his seven pigs without a contest. He even accompanied them to Iroda, and aided them to obtain the hound-whelp.

Meanwhile the fame of the successes of the sons of Turenn had come to Erin, and Luga of the Long Arms cast a Druidical spell over them, so that they quite forgot the cooking-spit and the three shouts on a hill, and came back to Erin thinking that they had fulfilled their 'eric.' But when Luga saw their spoils, he reminded them of the unfulfilled part of the compact, and the heroes had to set out again with heavy hearts, for they knew that Luga desired their death. When Brian got to the Island of Fincara, which lies beneath the sea, his beauty so pleased the warlike women that they gave him a cooking-spit without any trouble. Now all that was left to the heroes to do was to shout the three shouts on Midkena's hill. They sailed out into the north till they came to it, and there they fought desperately with Midkena and his sons, and overcame and killed them. But they were wounded themselves nigh unto death, and with the greatest difficulty they raised three feeble shouts on Midkena's hill. Then, wounded as they were, they sailed back to Erin, and implored Luga to let them taste of the apples of Hisberna, that they might recover. But Luga taunted them with the murder of his father, and would be content with nothing short of their death; so they died, and the blood of Kian was avenged.

While Nuada's silver hand was making, his place as king was taken by a regent named Bres. But when the silver hand was finished, Bres had to resign, to his great wrath; and he left the country and roused up a huge host of Fomorians under Balor of the Mighty Blows, and invaded Ireland, and was totally defeated. Balor of the Mighty Blows slew the poor silver-handed monarch, and was slain in his turn by Luga Long-Arms. Then Luga became king himself, and reigned long and happily, and many Tuatha de Danann reigned after him. But their time came at last to be overthrown by a fifth set of invaders—the Milesians, the sons of Milidh. The Milesians were an Eastern race, whom hoar tradition had set seeking a destined island; and they pursued the star of their destiny, the fine-eyed Ull-Erin, to the Irish shore. But they had no small trouble to win their way; the Tuatha de Danann kept them off as long as they could by spells and incantations, which wrapped the Milesian fleet in thick folds of impenetrable mist, and shook it with storms, and tossed the ships together on writhing waves. In that fierce tempest of dark enchantments many of the sons of Milidh perished; but they effected a landing at last, and carried all before them, and drove the De Danann into the fastnesses of the hills; and the Milesian leaders, Heber and Heremon, divided the island between them. They quarrelled about the division soon after, and Heremon killed Heber and took the whole island to himself—a Milesian version of Romulus. To this period belongs the second sorrowful tale of Erin—the tale of the fate of the children of Lir.

After the battle of Tailltenn, in which the Milesians won Ireland, the defeated Tuatha de Danann of the five provinces met together and chose Bove Derg king over them all. Lir, of Shee Finnalia, alone refused to acknowledge the new monarch, and retired to his own country. Some of the chieftains called for vengeance on Lir, but Bove Derg resolved to win his allegiance by friendship. He offered him the choice of his three foster-daughters—Eve, Eva, and Alva—in marriage. Lir relented, recognised the authority of Bove Derg, and married Eve, who bore him one daughter, Finola, and three sons, Aed, Ficia, and Conn. Eve died. Lir was for a time inconsolable, but on the advice of Bove Derg he married the second foster-daughter, Eva. The new stepmother, after the fashion of fairy tales, grew jealous of Lir's love for his children, and, like the woman in the German folk-story, turned them into swans. Mere metamorphosis did not content her; she laid this further doom on the children of Lir—that they must pass three hundred years on the smooth Lake Darvan, three hundred years on the wild Sea of Moyle, and yet three hundred more on the Western Sea. Nor was the spell to be loosened until the sound of a Christian bell was first heard in Erin. The only mitigation of their sufferings was the privilege of retaining their human voices. The wicked stepmother was punished by Bove Derg by being turned into a demon of the air; but the children of Lir had to dree their weird for the nine appointed centuries until the coming of Christianity, when they were disenchanted by St. Kemoc. In their human form they were very old; the saint baptized them, and they died and went to heaven.

What shall be said of the hundred and eighteen kings of the Milesian race? Which of those crowned figures is Tighearnmas, who first taught the Irish the worship of idols, and who distinguished his people into different ranks by the different hues of their garments? Or the wise Ollav Fodhla? Or that Cimbaoth, of whom the good chronicler Tighernach, Abbot of Clonmacnoise, wrote that all the Irish records before him were uncertain?—a respectable antiquity enough, if we might but take this Cimbaoth and his deeds for granted; for Pythagoras had just been crowned in the sixteeth Olympiad, and Numa Pompilius was still listening to the sweet counsels of the nymph Egeria in the cave celebrated by Juvenal, when Cimbaoth reigned.

Cimbaoth built the Palace of Emania. Ugaine Mor laid all Ireland under solemn oath, fearful as the ancient pledge by Styx; for he bound them by the visible and invisible elements to respect the rule of his race. But the oath was like thin air, and bound no one. Ugaine's son Lorc, and Lorc's son Oileel Ainey, were slain by Lorc's younger brother Corvac. But Corvac did not slay the grandson Lara; for the boy feigned idiocy, and the cruel king spared him—to his own doom; for the boy was brought up by a faithful harper, and in the fulness of time married a king's fair daughter, and passed over to France, and brought thence an army of stout Gaulish spearmen, and came back to his own, and slew Corvac, and founded a mighty line. One of his most famous descendants was Yeoha, surnamed the 'Sigher' for the sorrows he endured. For he married a fairy bride, whom he loved tenderly; but after a time there came a stranger from the land of the fairies, and bore her back to the fairy world, and with her went all the joy of Yeoha's life. Then his three sons rose in shameful rebellion against him, and were all slain, and their heads were laid at their father's feet. Good cause for sighing had Yeoha. But he was not all unhappy. His fairy bride had borne him a fairy daughter, the beautiful and gifted Meave, famous in Irish chronicles, and destined to fame through all the world as Queen Mab. Meave was a fierce, warlike woman, a very Semiramis of early Irish story. She married three husbands, and quarrelled with them all. In her reign occurred a battle between two bulls, which is recounted by the bards with all Homeric gravity. Meave lived a hundred years, and waged war with a great hero, Cucullin, and at last the fierce queen died and passed away. To her time belongs the third of the sorrowful tales of Erin—the story of Deirdri, the beautiful daughter of the bard Felemi, doomed at her birth to bring woe to Ulster.

Conor Mac Nessa, the King of Ulster, adopted her, kept her secluded, like Danæ, in a guarded place—not so well guarded but that she was once seen by Naesi, son of Usna. Naesi fell in love with her, and she with him. He carried her off with the aid of his two brothers, Anli and Ardan. Conor offered to pardon them if they came back to Emania, and in the end they did agree to return, escorted by a legion of soldiers under Fiachy, a gallant young noble. As they approached Emania, Deirdri, whose heart forebode evil, declared that she saw a blood-red cloud hanging in the distant sky. Her fears were well founded. When they drew near the king's capital, another noble, Durthacht, with another escort, came from Conor, and called upon Fiachy to yield him his charge. Fiachy suspected the treachery, refused to yield up the sons of Usna and the beautiful Deirdri, put them into a palace, and guarded it with his troops. It was his duty, he said, to show that the sons of Usna had not trusted in vain to the king's word or his good faith. Then Durthacht began the assault. The sons of Usna wished to surrender themselves, but Fiachy would not allow this—would not even permit them to take any share in the defence; it was his duty, and his alone. Then the sons of Usna and Deirdri withdrew into the palace, and Deirdri and Naesi played chess, and Anli and Ardan looked on while the battle raged outside. This battle deserves a place in story with the fierce strife in the halls of Attila which ends the

'Niebelungen Lied.' All through the bloody struggle the sons of Usna seemed intent alone upon the game they were playing, and as defence after defence of the palace was taken they remained unmoved, till at last Fiachy was killed, and the enemy rushed in and slew the sons of Usna at the board, and carried off Deirdri to Conor. But the king had no joy of her, for she killed herself soon after.

Meave's descendants ruled till the reign of Fiacha Finnolaidh, when there occurred a revolt of some tribes called the Attacotti, under a leader nicknamed 'Cat-Head.' They slew the king, and placed Cat-Head on his throne. After his death the rightful heirs came back, and the earth showed its approval by bountiful produce; fruitful meadows, fishful rivers, and many-headed woods proclaimed the joy of the Irish earth at the return of its true lords. But the Attacotti rose again and killed a rightful king, and a curse came upon the earth, and it was fruitless and cornless and fishless, till once again a king of the old race, Tuathal, seized the throne from the usurpers, and pledged the people by sun and moon and elements to leave the sceptre untroubled to his posterity. Tuathal then took a piece of land from each of the four provinces, and formed the kingdom of Meath to be the dwelling of the Ard-righ; and he built there four painted palaces, one for the king of each province.

Conn of the Hundred Fights, beloved of the bards, is the next famous king. After Conn's death the land passed to a usurper, Mac Con, for a time only, to return to the most famous of the early kings, Cormac Mac Art, in whose reign the Feni flourished. The Feni are strange and shadowy figures, Ossianic ghosts, moving in dusky vales and along hillsides clothed with echoing woods and seamed with the many-coloured sides of roaring streams; or by the angry sea, where the screaming sea-bird wings his flight towards the dark rolling heavens, where the awful faces of other times look out from the clouds, and the dread deities keep their cloudy halls, and the nightly fires burn. It is a land of mists and rains, through which the figures of the heroes loom gigantic. They are the kings of shaggy boars, the dwellers on battle's wing. They joy in the chase with their grey, rough-eared dogs about them. They rush against each other in war like the murmur of many waters, clashing their iron shields and shouting their surly songs; they remember the deeds of the days of old, and deaths wander like shadows over their fiery souls. Shadowy Death floats over the hosts, and rejoices at the frequent victims. When a hero falls, his soul goes forth to his fathers in their stormy isle, where they pursue boars of mist along the skirts of winds. Women, white-bosomed and beautiful, move like the music of songs through these antique tales, loving and beloved by heroes and kings of heroes.

Many of the stories have for their hero Finn, the son of Coul, the Fingal of the Scottish Ossian. Around him are his Feni, who stand in the same relation to him that the twelve peers do to Charlemagne, or the Knights of the Round Table to Arthur. Oisin, the sweet singer; Oscar, his glorious son, the Roland of the Feni; Dermat, of whom it might be said, as of Malory's Launcelot, that he was 'the truest lover of a sinful man that ever loved woman;' Dering, the beloved of Finn, and Kylta, the leader of the Clan Ronan; Conan, the comic glutton, of craven spirit and bitter tongue, a more grotesque Thersites; Fergus Finnvel, the warrior poet, reminding one of the Fiddler Knight in the 'Niebelungen Lied;' Ligna, the swift-footed; Gaul, the leader of the Clan Morna, whose enmity to the Clan Baskin made the battle of Gawra the Roncesvalles of the Feni. These are all heroes, going through all dangers, ever ready to do and to suffer bravely, battling with all the powers of darkness, loyal to each other, tender and courteous with women, gallant and goodly men, models of an early chivalry. Nor are Finn's famous dogs to be forgotten—Brann and Skolan, the companions of all his huntings and all his dangers.

Finn himself is a marvellous figure. In his youth he, like Theseus, destroyed all sorts of fearful monsters. He had also the privilege on occasion of knowing the future. His hair was grey through enchantment long before old age had clawed him in its clutch. Two fair sisters had loved him, and one of them said to the other that she could never love a man with grey hair. Then the other sister, despairing of winning Finn herself, lured him into an enchanted pool, which turned him into a withered old man. The angry Feni forced her to restore to their leader his youth, but his hair remained grey always.

The people of Lochlann, in the north of Europe, invaded Ireland with a mighty fleet, but were wholly routed by the Feni under Finn, in a battle in which Oscar, the son of Oisin, greatly distinguished himself. The enemy were routed with great slaughter, their king was slain, and his young son, Midac was taken prisoner. Finn brought up Midac in the ranks of the Feni, and treated him like a comrade; but Midac was always meditating revenge. At last, after fourteen years, Midac induced Sinsar of Greece and the Three Kings of the Torrent, to come secretly to Ireland with a mighty host, and they waited in a palace in an island of the Shannon, below where Limerick now is. Then Midac lured Finn, and many of the bravest of the Feni, who were on a hunting excursion, into a dwelling of his, the Palace of the Quicken Trees, as the mountain-ashes were called. The palace was enchanted, and once in it the heroes found themselves unable to get out, or even to move. So they set themselves to sing, in slow union, the Dord-Fian, the war-song of their race, while waiting death. But the party of Feni whom Finn had left behind him when he went to the Palace of the Quicken Trees began to grow anxious, and Ficna, Finn's son, and Innsa, his foster-brother, set out to look for them. When the pair came near the Palace of the Quicken Trees they heard the strains of the Dord-Fian; so they came close, and Finn heard them, and calling out, told them how he and his companions were trapped and waiting death, and that nothing could free them from enchantment but the blood of the Three Kings of the Torrent. Luckily for Finn, the only way to get to the Palace of the Quicken Trees from the palace of the island where Midac and the foreigners were lay over a narrow ford, where one man

might well keep a thousand at stand. This ford Ficna
and Innsa defended against desperate odds for long
enough. Innsa was first slain, and Ficna is engaged in
a desperate struggle with Midac, when Dermat appears
on the scene. The Feni who were at the hill were
growing impatient for the return of Ficna and Innsa,
so Oisin sent Dermat and Fatha to look for them. As
they approached the Palace of the Quicken Trees they
heard the noise of fighting at the ford. Then they ran
like the wind to the hill-brow over the river, and looking across in the dim moonlight, saw the whole ford
heaped with the bodies of the slain, and Ficna and Mildac fighting to the death. Dermat hurled his spear
and pierced Midac, who struck Ficna dead, and fell
dead himself. Then Dermat and Fatha defended the
ford against reinforcements of foreigners, and Dermat
soon killed the Three Kings of the Torrent, and undid
the spell that held Finn and his friends. Then all the
Feni came together, and the foreigners were routed
with great slaughter; the King of Greece and his son
were both slain, and the remnant of the enemy fled to
their ships in confusion and sailed away.

The friendship of Dermat and Finn was unfortunately
broken for a woman's sake. Finn sought the daughter
of Cormac Mac Art, the beautiful Grania, in marriage,
but the beautiful Grania had long loved the fair-faced
Dermat, in secret. When she saw herself about to be
wedded to Finn, no longer a young man, she told her
love to Dermat, and besought him to carry her away
from Finn. At first, Dermat, loyal to his king, refused,
though he was indeed deeply in love with the beautiful
Grania, but Grania placed him under 'gesa,' a kind of
mysterious command which heroes were supposed never
to disobey, to marry her and carry her off. Dermat,
in despair, consulted with his bravest comrades, with
Kylta, and Oscar, and Dering, and Oisin himself, and
all agreed that Finn would never forgive him, but that
he was bound to go with Grania and take the risk. So
go he did, and fled with her far from the court of King
Cormac. But great indeed was the wrath of Finn, and
for long after he pursued Dermat and Grania from

place to place, always seeking to have Dermat killed, and always failing, owing to the skill of Dermat. All the sympathy of the Feni went with Dermat, and not with Finn. Very beautifully the old story celebrates the love of Dermat and Grania, and the gallant deeds Dermat did for her sake. At last, weary of the pursuit, Finn consented to pardon Dermat, but in his heart he always cherished hatred against him, and when Dermat was wounded to death by a boar, Finn refused him the drink of water which from his hand would prove a cure. So Dermat died, to the great sorrow and anger of all the Feni. The story is one of the most beautiful, as it is the saddest, of the old Irish legends.

Oisin, the last of the Feni, is said to have outlived all his companions by many centuries, and to have told of them and their deeds to St. Patrick. He had married a beautiful girl. who came to wed him from a country across the sea, called Tirnanoge, and there he dwelt, as he thought, for three, but as it proved, for three hundred, years. At the end of that time there came on him a great longing to see Erin again, and after much entreaty his fair wife allowed him to return, on the one condition that he never dismounted from a white steed which she gave him. When he got to Ireland he found that the Feni had long passed away, and that only the distant fame of them lingered in men's minds. Of course he dismounts from the horse—how many fairy tales would have ended happily if their heroes had only done as they were told!—and the horse straightway flies away, and then the curse of his old age comes upon Oisin, who falls to the ground an old withered, blind man, doomed never again to go back to Tirnanoge and his fair wife and his immortal youth. St. Patrick was now in Ireland, and often spoke with Oisin, who never tired of telling of the heroes of his youth, and wondering that death could ever have laid hands upon their bright beauty. Bitterly he complained of the sound of the Christian bell and the hymns of the Christian clerics, which had enchanted and destroyed the Feni. 'There is no joy in your strait cells,' Oisin wails. 'There are no women among you, no cheerful music;' and he laments for the joys of his youth, the songs of the blackbirds, the sound of the wind, the cry of the hounds let loose, the wash of water against the sides of ships, and the clash of arms, and the sweet voices of his youth's compeers.

CHAPTER II.

CHRISTIANITY.

THE authorities for all this wonderful fanciful legend, for all this pompous record of visionary kings and heroes, are to be found in the ancient Irish manuscripts, in the Ossianic songs, in the annals of Tighernach, of Ulster, of Inis Mac Nerinn, of Innisfallen, and of Boyle, in the 'Chronicum Scotorum,' the books of Leinster and of Ballymote, the Yellow Book of Lecain, and the famous annals of the Four Masters, which Michael O'Clerigh, the poor friar of the Order of St. Francis, compiled for the glory of God and the honour of Ireland. They are interpreted and made accessible to us by scholars and writers like O'Curry, and Ferguson, and Mr. P. W. Joyce, and Mr. Standish O'Grady. These and others have translated enough to show that the Irish manuscripts enclose a store of romantic records and heroic tales that will bear comparison well with the legends and the folk lore of any other country. There is yet much to do in the way of translating and popularizing these old Irish legends, and it may well be hoped and believed that Irish scholarship will prove itself equal to the task. But these antique tales are not history.' We cannot even say whether they have an historical basis. It matters very little. They are beautiful legends, in any case, and, like the tale of the Trojan War, and the records of the Seven Kings of Rome, they may be believed or not, according to the spirit of their student. It is more probable than not that they have a foundation of truth. Recent discoveries in the Troad have given an historical position to the siege of Troy; and the Irish chronicles have no worse claim to respect, as historic documents, than the rhapsodies of the Homeric singer. But modern historians prefer to leave the Tuatha de Danann and the Milesians undisturbed in their shadowy kingdom, and content themselves with suggesting that Ireland was at first inhabited by a Turanian race, and that there were Celtic and Teutonic immigrations.

The social organization of pre-Christian Ireland shows many remarkable signs of civilization, especially in its treament of women, who were invested with a respect and dignity not common in the early history of races. In the legends, women receive always from men a tender and gracious submission that rivals the chivalry of the Arthurian romances; and there is every reason to believe that this was not confined to legend. The married woman was regarded as the equal of her husband no less than if she had lived in Rome, and repeated on her wedding-day the famous formula, 'Ubi tu Caius ego Caia.' The religion seems to have been a form of sun-worship, regulated by Druids, and not, it is said— though this is strongly contested—unaccompanied with human sacrifices. The people were divided into septs, composed of families bearing the name of their founder. The headman of each family served the chief of the sept, and each septal king in his turn recognised the authority of the Ard-Righ, or chief king. All chieftainships, and the offices of Druid and of Brehon, or lawgiver, were elective. During the life of each chief, his successor, called the 'Tanist,' was chosen from the same family. Land was held by each sept in common, without any feudal condition, and primogeniture was unknown. Legitimate or illegitimate sons were partners with their father, and after his death took equal shares of his holding. The Brehon criminal laws punished almost every offence by more or less heavy fines. Agriculture was in its infancy. Wealth lay in cattle, pigs, sheep, and horses. Ore and slaves were exported to the Mediterranean countries from the earliest times. The people dwelt in wattled houses, and their palaces were probably only of painted wood built on dyked and palisaded hills; but they could build strong fortresses and great sepulchral chambers, and raise vast cromlechs over their warrior dead. Whether the round towers which are still the wonder of many parts of Ireland were built by them or by the early Christians, and for what purpose, is still a subject of fierce controversy among archæologists. Diodorus Siculus would seem to refer to them in a passage in which he speaks of an island of the size of Sicily, in the ocean over against Gaul, to the north, whose people were said to have a great affection for the Greeks from old times, and to build curious temples of round form. Whether they built the round towers or no, the early Irish were skilled in the working of gold ornaments, and in the manufacture of primitive weapons. They seem to have known the art of writing early, and to have had a strange alphabet of their own, called Ogham, from a shadowy King Oghma, who was supposed to have invented it. It was written by cutting notches in wood and stone, and there has been no small discussion over the reading of it.

Authentic history begins with St. Patrick. Patrick had been carried as a slave from Gaul to Erin in his youth. He escaped to Rome and rose high in the Christian Church. But his heart was stirred with pity for his land of bondage, and about 432 he returned to Ireland, inspired by the hope of converting the country. He was not the first. Palladius had tried to convert Pagan Ierne already, but where Palladius failed, Patrick succeeded; and the complete conversion of Ireland is one of the most splendid triumphs of the early Church. Wherever the saint went, conviction and conversion followed. He had dreamed a strange dream while in Rome, in which an angel appeared to him, bearing a scroll, with the superscription, 'The voice of the Irish.' The voice of the Irish had called him, and the ears of the Irish were ready to accept his teaching: king after king, chieftain after chieftain, abandoned the worship of their ancient gods to become the servants of Christ. For more than sixty years Patrick wrestled with the old gods in Ireland and overthrew them. He had found Ireland Pagan, but when he died and gave

> 'His body to that pleasant country's earth,
> And his pure soul unto his captain Christ,
> Under whose colours he had fought so long.'

the spirit of Christianity was over the island, and the power of the old gods was gone for ever. He was buried in Saul, in the county of Down, but his spirit lived in the souls of his followers. Long after Patrick had been laid to rest, his disciples carried the cross of Christ to the gaunt Scottish Highlands, the lonely German pine-forests, the savage Gaulish settlements, to Britain, and the wild islands of the Northern Seas. The Irish monks wandered into the waste places of Ireland, and noble monasteries—the homes of religion and of learning—sprang up wherever they set their feet. The fathers of the Irish Church were listened to with reverence in the court of Charlemagne and in the Roman basilicas; and foreign ecclesiastics eagerly visited the homes of these men—the monasteries famous for their learning, their libraries, and their secure peace.

The island of the Sun-god had become the island of saints. To Ireland belong St. Columban, the reformer of the Gauls; St. Columbkill, the 'Dove of the Cell,' whose name has made Iona holy ground; St. Foelan; St. Killian, the apostle of Franconia; St. Aidan; St. Gall, the converter of Helvetia; and St. Boniface. One hundred and fifty-five Irish saints are venerated in the churches of Germany, forty-five in Gaul, thirty in Belgium, thirteen in Italy, and eight in Scandinavia. For a long time all Christendom looked upon Ireland as the favourite home of religion and of wisdom. Montalembert, in his great history of 'The Monks of the West,' has given a glowing account of the civilization and the culture of the Irish monasteries. There the arts were practised—music, architecture, and the working of metals. There the languages of Greece and Rome were studied with the passionate zeal which afterwards distinguished the Humanistic scholars of the revival of learning. The Irish monastic scholars carried their love for Greek so far that they even wrote the Latin of the Church books in the beloved Hellenic characters—and as we read we are reminded again of the old tradition of Greek descent—while, curiously enough, one of the oldest manuscripts of Horace in existence, that in the library of Berne, is written in Celtic characters, with notes and commentaries in the Irish language. It is worthy of remark that Montalembert says, that of all nations the Anglo-Saxons derived most profit from the teaching of the Irish schools, and that Alfred of England received his education in an Irish University.

With the lapse of time, however, and the disorders that came over the country during the struggles with the Danes, the organization of the Church suffered severely. In the twelfth century the irregularities that had crept into the Irish Church were brought before the notice of the Roman court. A synod, held at Kells, A.D. 1152, under the Papal Legate Paparo, formally incorporated the Irish Church into the ecclesiastical system of Rome. The Metropolitan Sees of Armagh, Cashel, Dublin, and Tuam, were created, with their Suffragan Sees, under the Primacy of the Archbishop of Armagh.

Towards the end of the eighth century the Danes made their first descent upon Irelend, and for a time established themselves in the country, expending their fiercest fury upon the Church of the West, and driving the Irish scholars to carry their culture and their philosophy to the great cities of the European Continent. The Irish chiefs, divided amongst themselves, were unable to oppose a common front to the enemy, and for more than a century the sea-kings held Ireland in subjection. At length a man arose who was more than a match for the sea-kings. Brian Boroimhe, brother of the King of Munster, raised an army against the Danes in 968, thoroughly defeated them, and reduced them to the condition of quiet dwellers in the seaport towns. But the master-spirit that the troublous time had conjured up was not content to remain the conqueror of the Danes alone. He was determined to become the sovereign of all Ireland. It was sheer usurpation, and many of the Irish chiefs opposed Brian; but he soon overcome their resistance, and in 1001 he was acknowledged as King of all Ireland. He made a just and wise king, and for twelve years reigned in triumph and in peace. Then the Danes in Ireland began to pluck up heart again. They sent for help to their kinsmen over sea, and the Vikings came across the Swan's Bath with a mighty fleet, and made war upon Brian. Brian was an old man now, but as fierce and brave and skilful as ever. He raised up all his power to meet the Danes, and completely defeated them after a bloody struggle at Clontarf, on Good Friday, 1014. Their bravest chiefs were slain, and their spirits sent to the Hall of Odin to drink ale with the goddesses of death, while all the hawks of heaven mourned for them. But the victorious Irish had to bewail their king, who, owing to the negligence of his guards, was killed in his tent towards the end of the fight by the Danish leader. This great defeat of the Danes put an end to any further dreams of a Danish invasion of Ireland, though it did not by any means destroy the influence that the Danes had already acquired in the island. They still held their own in the great seaport towns, and carried on fierce feuds with the native tribes, and in the slow processes of time became absorbed into and united with them. The death of Brian had a disastrous effect upon the condition of Ireland. The provinces that he had subjugated reasserted their independence; but his usurpation had shattered the supremacy of the old royal race, and the history of Ireland until the middle of the twelfth century is merely a melancholy succession of civil wars and struggles for the crown, upon which it would be alike painful and profitless to dwell.

CHAPTER III.

THE NORMAN CONQUEST.

IRELAND was now divided into four confederations of tribes. The O'Neils held Ulidia, which is now called Ulster; the O'Connors Conacia, or Connaught; the O'Briens and the M'Carthys Mononia, or Munster; and the Macmurroughs Lagenia, or Leinster—all under the paramount but often-disputed rule of a branch of the Ulster O'Neils. The royal demesne of Meath, the appanage of the Ulster family, which included Westmeath, Longford, and a part of King's County, was sometimes counted a fifth kingdom.

In the wild north, O'Neil, O'Donnel, O'Kane, O'Hara, O'Sheel, O'Carrol, were mighty names. On the northernmost peninsula, where the Atlantic runs into Lough Foyle and Lough Swilly, O'Dogherty reigned supreme. In Connaught, O'Rourke, O'Reilly, O'Kelly, O'Flaherty, O'Malley, O'Dowd, were lords. In Meath and Leinster, MacGeogeghan, O'Farrell, O'Connor, O'Moore, O'Brennan, Macmurrough ruled. In Munster, by the western shore, MacCarthy More held sway. MacCarthy Reagh swayed the south, by the pleasant waters of Cork Bay. O'Sullivan Beare was lord of the fair promontory between Bantry Bay and Kenmare River. O'Mahony reigned by roaring Water Bay. O'Donohue was chieftain by the haunted Killarney Lakes. McMahon ruled north of the Shannon. O'Loglin looked on Galway Bay.

All Ireland, with the exception of a few seaport towns where the Danes had settled, was in the hands of Irish chiefs of old descent and famous lineage. They quarrelled amongst themselves as readily and as fiercely as if they had been the heads of so many Greek states. The Danes had been their Persians; their Romans were now to come.

The whole story of Irish subjugation and its seven centuries of successive struggles begins with the carrying off of Devorgilla, wife of Tiernan O'Rorke, of Brefny, by a dissolute, brutal giant some sixty years old—Dermot Macmurrough, King of Leinster. We have a curious picture of him preserved in the writings of Giraldus Cambrensis, who knew him, and who was the first historian of the Irish invasion. 'Dermot was a man of tall stature and great body; a valiant and bold warrior in his nation. By constant halloaing and crying out his voice had become hoarse. He chose to be feared rather than loved; oppressed his nobility greatly, but greatly supported and advanced the poor and weak. To his own kindred he was rough and grievous, and hateful to strangers; he would be against all men, and all men were against him.' Such was the man who found the fair wife of the Lord of Brefny a willing victim. Alexander the Great was pleased to fancy that in ravaging the countries of the Great King he was still avenging the ancient quarrel for the rape of Helen. But Helen was not more fatal to Greeks and Easterns than Devorgilla, Erin's Helen, proved to the neighbouring islands that lie along the Irish Sea. Through ages of bloodshed and slaughter her country has indeed bled for her shame. There is a grim ironic mockery in the thought that two nations have been set for centuries in the bitterest hatred by the loves of a lustful savage and an unfaithful wife. One might well paraphrase the words of Shakespeare's Diomed in 'Troilus and Cressida,' and say that 'for every false drop in her bawdy veins an English life hath sunk; for every scruple of her contaminated carrion weight an Irishman been slain.' The Lord of Brefny made war upon his betrayer; Rory O'Connor, the last king of Ireland, espoused O'Rorke's cause, and Dermot fled the country. He hastened to Aquitaine, where Henry II. was then staying, and did him homage. Pope Adrian IV., known to England as Nicholas Breakspere, the only Englishman who ever sat in the seat of St. Peter, had given Henry II. a Bull of Authority over Ireland some years before, authority which Henry had not yet seen fit to exercise. Dermot's quarrel was Henry's opportunity. He allowed the treacherous fugitive to shark up a list of lawless resolutes from among the Norman barons in Wales, headed by Richard de Clare, Earl Pembroke, called 'Strongbow.' Ireland was invaded, Wexford seized, Waterford taken and sacked, and Eva, Dermot's daughter, married to Strongbow, as a further bond between the Lord of Leinster and the Norman adventurer. The superiority of the Norman arms and armour impressed the Irish chiefs and soldiery as the iron of Charlemagne's legions impressed the Huns. The Normans made a brave show, lapped in steel, with their pointed helms and shields, their surcoats gleaming with the *or* and *argent*, *gules* and *azure* of their heraldic bearings, their powerful weapons, and their huge war-horses. Beneath their floating pennons came their well-trained, well-armed soldiers, skilled to shoot with long-bow and cross-bow, well supplied with all the implements fit for the taking of cities that Roman ingenuity had devised and Norman craft perfected. The Irish galloglasses and kerns opposed to them, if not wholly unfamiliar with the use of mail, seldom indeed used it, and fought their fiercest, protected alone by the shirts of saffron-dye in which they delighted, while their weapons were in every respect inferior to those of the invaders. Naturally, the Normans were at first triumphant everywhere. They swarmed over the country, pushing their strange names and strange ways into the homes of the time-honoured septs. De Burgo in Connaught, FitzMaurice and FitzGerald in Kerry, in the land of the MacCarthy More; De Cogan, FitzStephen, and De la Poer along the southern coast; De Lacy in the north; all the cloud of De Grandisons, and De Montmorencies, and De Courcies, and Mandevilles, and FitzEustaces, who settled along the eastern coasts, and pushed their way inland—these were to be the new masters of men whose hearts were given in allegiance to the lords of the O and of the Mac.

But though the first flush of victory rested with the Normans, their hold over the country was for some time uncertain. Dermot, whose alliance was of great importance to the invaders, died suddenly a loathsome death. Henry seemed little inclined to lend his strength to the bold barons, whose successes made him jealous for his own authority over the island. He even ordered Strongbow to leave Ireland, a command that it was difficult to obey, for the Irish had plucked up heart of grace to turn upon their invaders, and were harassing them very effectually. They were reinforced, too, by their old enemies the Danes, whose seaport settlements the Normans had seized upon with scant courtesy, and between the two the adventurers were in a bad way. Strongbow took the opportunity of a momentary triumph of the Norman arms to return to England and make his peace with his jealous monarch. Henry pardoned him his delayed submission, and immediately secured the Norman grasp on Ireland by leading a large army across the Irish Sea on a 'Veni, vidi, vici,' visit, as Sir John Davies called it, writing of it some centuries later.

The armament overawed many of the Irish chieftains, who seem to have thought resistance to the master of such legions vain, and most of the Munster chieftains came in and swore allegiance. Rory O'Connor held out against the king; so did the Ulster chiefs; but Henry, content with what he gained, for the time let them alone, and proceeded to organize his new territory. He divided it into counties, and set up the royal law courts of Bench, Pleas, and Exchequer in Dublin, to afford the Norman settlers the privileges of English law. The natives were allowed to keep to their old Brehon laws, which dated from the earliest times, and were as unlike the English processes of jurisprudence as the Irish land system was unlike the feudal system now introduced.

Henry's stay in Ireland was abruptly cut short by a summons to appear before the Papal Legates in Normandy who were inquiring into the murder of Beckett. He left the island never to come back to it again. But he had done much to Normanize the country by making large and wholly illegal grants of Septal territory to his followers, leaving it to them to win and keep these gifts as best they could. With the sword the barons advanced their claims, and with the sword the Irish chieftains met them.

The story of Ireland from the first to the second Richard is one monotonous record of constant warfare between the Irish and the Normans, and of incessant strife between the rival Irish houses. The barons built great castles, and lived in them a life of rough self-reliance, very like that of the robber lords of the Rhine provinces in later centuries. Many of these domains were counties palatinate, that is to say their lords had the privilege of making their own laws with very little regard to the jurisdiction of the crown, and with absolute power of life and death. They ruled the tenants accordingly, with a queer mixture of Brehon and Norman law, after their own fashion. In the Norman towns, which were gradually established in the country under the protection of some one or other of the great barons, the language for a long time was only Norman French, and the customs as well. It was as if some town of pleasant Normandy had been taken bodily up and transported to Ireland, with its well-wardered ramparts, on which the citizens' wives and daughters walked of quiet evenings in times of peace, its busy crowded streets, thronged with citizens of all trades and crafts, marching sometimes gaily in their guilds, and ready at all times to drop awl or hammer, net or knife, and rush to arms to attack or to repel the Irish enemy. For outside the ramparts of these Norman towns on Irish earth, outside the last bastion of the baron's stronghold, lay the Irish, a separate and a hostile nation, ever attacked, and ever ready to attack. The return of the swallow was not surer in summer than the renewed outbreak of strife between Norman baron and Irish chief when once the winter had faded into spring. The baron took to the road like a last century highwayman: he swooped down upon the fields of the Irish; he seized upon the stores that they had placed in their churches and churchyards, as was their custom before they took to building castles themselves. The Irish retaliated whenever and wherever they could.

For long there was no sort of alliance between them. Only those who belonged to the 'five bloods' of the O'Neils of Ulster, the O'Connors of Connaught, the O'Briens of Thomond, the O'Melachlins of Meath, and the Macmurroughs of Leinster, could have audience in an English court. The killing of an Irishman or the violation of an Irishwoman by an English colonist was no crime.

Yet, with the slow advance of time the Norman settlers began to succumb to Irish influences. The hostilities lessened, the hatreds waned. The Norman barons began to find peace better than war, and love fairer than feud. They took to themselves wives from among the daughters of the Irish chiefs. By degrees they abandoned their knightly trappings, their Norman names, and their foreign speech, to adopt instead the Irish dress, names, language, and law. A Burke became a M'William, a Fitzmaurice became a M'Morice, and a Bermingham became a M'Yoris. The transformed barons aspired to be independent Irish chieftains like their new allies; in time they came to be known as 'more Irish than the Irish themselves.'

The English Government witnessed with jealous anger this curious process of assimilation, and strove at intervals to stay its course. A statute passed in 1295 prohibited in vain the adoption of the Irish garb by Norman settlers. The English had not the power to enforce such restrictive laws; they had not even the strength to protect such of the settlers as were willing to abide by their own Norman ways and words. These were forced in self-defence into association and alliance with the Irish chiefs, who were gradually regaining their control over the country.

After the English defeat at Bannockburn, the Irish chiefs at once rose in revolt against England. Edward Bruce, brother of the victorious Scottish king, came over to Ireland in 1315, and was heartily welcomed, not by the native Irish alone, but by many of the Anglo-Irish nobles. Edward Bruce was crowned as king at Dundalk, and for a short time the insurrection carried all before it, and the Anglo-Irish lords who had not joined the rebellion were put to great straits to defend themselves. The English Government made a desperate effort, raised a large army under Sir John de Bermingham, which completely defeated the allied Scotch, Irish, and Anglo-Irish forces in a battle near Dundalk, in which Edward Bruce himself was killed. But the victory was dearly bought. The loyal Anglo-Irish had learned to their cost that they could not count for safety on the protection of the home Government, and that security was more easily attained by amalgamation with the Irish. The Irishizing process went on more vigorously than ever. The conversion of Norman barons into Irish chiefs with Irish names waxed day by day. The condition of the English settlers who remained unchanged in the midst of such changes became desperate indeed.

Something had to be done. In 1356 it was proclaimed that no one born in Ireland should hold any of the king's towns or castles. This proved ineffectual, and sterner measures were resorted to eleven years later, at the Parliament held in Kilkenny, in 1367. The Norman Parliament in Ireland was originally a council of the barons, prelates, and the 'faithful;' but it had grown with time into greater importance. The Upper House consisted of lay peers, abbots, priors, and bishops; the Lower House of the knights of the shires and burgesses. Many of the lay peers claimed and received exemption from attendance, and the abbots, priors, and bishops generally sent their proctors in their places, till the practice grew up of summoning two proctors from each diocese, who sat with the knights and burgesses in the Lower House, and claimed to be members of the legislature. Most of the shires were in the hands of the Irish, and returned no members. Burgesses were summoned from a few towns, many not being elected by the freemen of the city, but receiving the royal writ personally, by name. It met at irregular intervals, sometimes at Dublin, sometimes at Kilkenny, and sometimes at Drogheda, at the summons of the king's lieutenant, or his deputy.

The Parliament of Kilkenny inflicted heavy penalties

on all English who adopted Irish names, speech, or customs. The Norman who dared to marry an Irish wife was to be half-hanged, shamefully mutilated, disembowelled alive, and forfeit his estate. The fostering of Norman with Irish children, and the maintenance of Irish bards, were alike sternly prohibited. But at the time the English Government had not the power to enforce these statutes, which only served to further exasperate the Irish and the Anglo-Irish.

Richard II. was in Ireland with a large army, determined to reduce the country to obedience, when the news of Bolingbroke's landing at Ravenspurgh called him back to his death. The struggles of the Houses of the White and the Red Rose occupied Ireland as well as England. Anglo-Irish lords crossed the sea to fight for York and Lancaster by the side of the King-maker or Clifford of Cumberland. In Ireland the two greatest houses took opposite sides. The Butlers of East Munster, the Lords of Ormonde, who swayed Tipperary and Kilkenny, plucked a sanguine rose with young Somerset; while the Geraldines of both the Desmond and Kildare branches loved no colours, and cropped a pale and angry rose with Plantagenet.

The story of the house of Geraldine is one of the most romantic in all Irish history. The Geraldines were descended from the two brothers Maurice and William Fitzgerald, who came to Ireland at the heels of Strongbow. Through varying fortunes—at one time the whole house was nearly exterminated by MacCarthy More—they had risen to a proud position of rule in Ireland. They owned all the broad lands from Maynooth to Lixnaw; their followers swarmed everywhere, bearing a 'G' on their breast in token that they owed their hearts to the Geraldines.

Moore has made famous the story of Thomas, the sixth earl, who, 'by the Fial's wave benighted, no star in the sky,' was lighted by love to the door of a retainer's cottage. The poet fancies that as the chieftain crossed the threshold, some ominous voice whispered that there was ruin before him. If he loved he was lost. Love and ruin did indeed await the Geraldine across the threshold. The retainer had a beautiful daughter, and 'love came and brought sorrow too soon in his train' for Thomas of Kildare. He married the peasant girl, and was outlawed by his stately family, and went to France with his humble love, and died, a poor but a happy man, at Rouen, many years later.

After Bosworth Battle had placed Henry VII. on the throne of Richard of Gloucester, the new king was too busy with his new kingdom to give much thought to Ireland. The English colony was in a bad way there. It was reduced to the county of Dublin and parts of Meath, Louth, and Kildare. The greater part of the island was entirely in the hands of Irish chieftains, who exacted tribute from the English, and scornfully set at naught the continued and meaningless renewals of the statutes of Kilkenny. Henry at first left Ireland alone. He was ever content to leave the Geraldine control of the country unquestioned, although the Geraldines had been so defiantly Yorkist, and though not a few followers of the house had painted their own white roses red with their own blood on many an English field. They were Yorkist still. When Lambert Simnel came over to Ireland, pretending to be the son of false, fleeting, perjured Clarence, the Geraldines rallied round him with warm support and sympathy. When this image of a king was swept from the throne to the kitchen, Perkin Warbeck took his place, claimed to be the Duke of York whom Gloucester had murdered in the tower, and he, too, found Geraldine aid and maintenance. Henry had now learnt something of the strength of Irish disaffection in the hands of the Irish chiefs, and prepared to crush it out more subtly than by the sword. We have seen what the Irish Parliament was like: a poor thing enough in itself, but at worst containing the principles of a representative system. This system Henry resolved to destroy. Three centuries had passed since the Norman banners had first floated over the Irish fields, and in all that time no attempt had been made to force the English laws upon the Irish Septs, or to interfere with the self-government of the Norman settlers. Now, in 1494, Henry sent over Sir Edward

Poynings, as Lord Deputy, with an army at his back, to change altogether the relationship between the two islands. Poynings summoned a Parliament at Drogheda, at which the famous measure known as Poynings's Act was passed. This Act established that all English laws should operate in Ireland, and that the consent of the Privy Council of England was necessary for all Acts of the Irish Parliament. These measures at once deprived Ireland of all claim to independent government. Henceforward she was to be the helpless dependent of the conquering country. But the loss of liberty did not destroy the Irish desire for freedom; it rather gave it an additional incentive to action.

Ireland being thus soldered close to England, Henry was content to leave the government of the country in the hands of its most powerful man. 'All Ireland,' men said, 'was not a match for the Earl of Kildare.' 'Then let the Earl of Kildare govern all Ireland,' said Henry VII., and gave the rule of Ireland into his hands. He had been the most potent spirit in Ireland under the old system; to confirm his power under the new seemed to the astute Henry the surest means of securing his allegiance and the quiet dependence of Ireland.

His successor, the Eighth Henry, looked on the Geraldine power with grave jealousy. The control of the island was practically in the hands of the Earls of Kildare and their followers, and was drifting day by day further from the control and supremacy of England. What use were statutes of Kilkenny and Poynings's Acts if the country was under the command of an Anglo-Irish house who defied the authority of England? His jealousy of the Geraldines was fostered by Wolsey, who was considerably under the influence of the House of Ormonde, the bitter enemies of the Geraldines. Gerald, the ninth earl, son of Henry VII.'s deputy, was summoned to England. He was at once thrown into the Tower, and false news of his execution was sent to Dublin. His son, Lord Thomas Fitzgerald, 'Silken Thomas,' as he was commonly called by his people, from the splendour of his dress, displayed no silken spirit. He raised at once a desperate revolt against the

king, but his forces were shattered by the English ar
tillery, brought thus into Irish warfare for the first
time. He and his five uncles were compelled to surrender. They were sent to London, to the Tower,
where the Earl of Kildare had died of a broken heart,
and they were all hanged at Tyburn. Only one of their
kin, a boy of twelve, a son of the Earl of Kildare by his
second wife, escaped from the slaughter of his race to
Rome, to found again the fortunes of his house. 'The
dying Gracchus,' said Mirabeau, 'flung dust to heaven,
and from that dust sprang Marius.' From the blood
of the Geraldines arose the great house of Desmond and
Tyrone, which at one time seemed likely to establish
the independence of Ireland.

Henry's next act was to confiscate the Church lands
in Ireland as he had done in England. How this was
done we may learn in the melancholy words of the Four
Masters: 'They broke down the the monasteries, and
sold their roofs and bells from Arran of the Saints to
the Iccian Sea. . . They burned the images, shrines,
and relics. . . the staff of Jesus, which had been in the
hand of St. Patrick.' A Parliament was summoned at
Dublin, at which for the first time some Irish chieftains were to be seen sitting by the English lords at the
national assembly. These chiefs agreed to hold their
land of the king by English law, to come to the king's
courts for justice, to attend Parliament, to send their
sons to be educated at the English court, and to renounce the authority of the Pope. The Parliament
conferred on Henry and his successors the title of King
instead of Lord Paramount of Ireland.

Under Edward, the chiefs who dwelt in Leix, Offaly,
Fercal, and Ely, in the central plain of Ireland, of
whom the O'Moores and O'Connors were chief, showed
signs of revolt. They were formidable and warlike,
and Henry VIII. had thought it well worth his while to
keep them quiet by subsidy. With the news of his
death they may have thought that an opportunity of
some kind had come; but whether they intended rebellion or not, the Government acted on the assumption
that they did, and crushed them before they had time

to move, captured their chiefs, laid waste their settlements, and finally confiscated their lands, and planted them with English settlers. The dispossessed Irish drove the settlers out after nine years of ceaseless warfare. Then the Government put forth its strength, shot down the obnoxious natives wherever they could get at them, hunted them as outlaws, and at last practically exterminated them. Mary was by this time on the throne. A part of Offaly, Fercal, and Ely was converted into King's County; Leix, another portion of Offaly, and Upper Ossory, became Queen's County. In the settlement of these two counties we may see the beginnings of those plantation schemes, which were to be carried on, on so large a scale, by the succeeding English rulers, whether Tudor, Stuart, or Puritan.

CHAPTER IV.

ELIZABETH.

The Reformation begun under Henry VIII. was carried out with pitiless determination under Edward VI., and was met by the Catholics with unflinching opposition. Under Mary there was a period of respite, but the strife was renewed with greater fierceness in the suceeeding reign. As authentic Irish history begins with St. Patrick, so with Elizabeth modern Irish history may be said to begin. The principles of the Reformation had only served to deepen the hostility, already deep enough, between the Irish chiefs and the English crown. It had also served to unite the Catholic Anglo-Irish with the Catholic native Irish as they had never been united before. The English Act of Uniformity had not yet been registered by a Parliament. Elizabeth, in January, 1560, summoned a carefully chosen and obedient Parliament, which repealed the Catholic Acts passed by Mary, and passed the Act of Uniformity, which made the new liturgy compulsory. Many of the bishops accepted the situation; those who refused, and who were within Elizabeth's power, were deprived; those outside the pale and its power trusted in their isolation and defied the new measures. The seizures of Henry and Edward had impoverished the Irish Church, but the spirit of the Church was unbroken. On hillsides and by hedges the mendicant friars still preached the faith of their fathers in their fathers' native tongue, and wherever they went they found a people eager to hear and to honour them, resolute to oppose the changes that came in the name of Henry, of Edward, and of Elizabeth from across the sea.

At her accession, Elizabeth was too much occupied with foreign complications to pay much heed to Ireland. Trouble first began in a conflict between the feudal laws and the old Irish law of Tanistry. Con O'Neil, Earl of Tyrone, had taken his title from Henry VIII., subject to the English law of succession; but when Con died, the clan O'Neil, disregarding the English principle of hereditary succession, chose Shane O'Neil, an illegitimate son of Con, and the hero of his Sept, to be The O'Neil. Shane O'Neil at once put himself forward as the champion of Irish liberty, the supporter of the Irish right to rule themselves in their own way and pay no heed to England. Under the pretence of governing the country, Elizabeth overran it with a soldiery who, as even Mr. Froude acknowledges, lived almost universally on plunder, and were little better than bandits. The time was an appropriate one for a champion of Irish rights. Shane O'Neil boldly stood out as sovereign of Ulster, and pitted himself against Elizabeth. She tried to have him moved by assassination. When this failed she tried to temporise. Shane was invited to England, where the courtly gentlemen who hovered about Elizabeth stared over their spreading ruffs in wonder at Shane the Proud and his wild followers in their saffron-stained shirts and rough cloaks, with great battleaxes in their hands. They sharpened their wits upon his haughty bearing, his scornful speech, and his strange garb. But his size and strength made great impression on the Queen, and for the moment an amicable arrangement seemed to be arrived at. For many years there had been a steady immigration of Scots from Argyleshire into Antrim, who had often served Shane O'Neil as mercenaries. These Scotch settlers seem to have been regarded with dislike by the Crown; at all events, it was part of the compact with Shane that he should reduce them, and reduce them he did, with no light or sparing hand. But the fierce King of Ulster was by far too powerful to please Elizabeth long. Her agents induced other tribes to rise against him. Shane fought bravely against his fate, but he was defeated, put to flight, and murdered by his enemies, the Scots of Antrim, in whose strongholds he madly sought refuge. His head was struck off, and sent to adorn the walls of Dublin Castle. His lands were declared forfeit, and his vassals vassals of the Crown. English soldiers of fortune were given grants from Shane's escheated territory, but when they attempted to settle they were killed by the O'Neils. Others came in their place, under Walter Devereux, Earl of Essex, and did their best to simplify the process of colonization by exterminating the O'Neils, men, women, and children, wherever they could be got at. After two years of struggle, Essex was compelled to abandon his settlement. But other colonizers were not disheartened. Some West of England gentlemen, under Peter Carew, seized on Cork, Limerick, and Kerry, and sought to hold them by extirpating the obnoxious natives.

Against these English inroads the great Geraldine League was formed. In the reign of Mary, that boy of twelve whom Henry VIII. had not been able to include in the general doom of his house had been allowed to return to Ireland, and to resume his ancestral honours. Once more the Geraldines were a great and powerful family in Ireland. But their strength had again awakened the alarm of the English Government. The Earl of Desmond and his brother had been summoned to England and cast into the Tower. Their cousin, James Fitzmaurice of Desmond, now began to unite the Geraldines against Carew and his companions, and fought them and those sent to help them for two years. They were of course defeated, not however so badly but that Elizabeth was willing not only to receive their submission, but to release Desmond and his brother from the Tower and send them back to Ireland. James Fitzmaurice Fitzgerald went into voluntary exile, wandering from capital to capital of the Catholic Continental Powers, seeking aid and assistance for his cherished Geraldine League. The Geraldines and their companion chiefs got encouragement in Rome and pledges from Spain, and they rose again under the Earl of Desmond and Sir James Fitzmaurice Fitzgerald. At first they had some successes. They had many wrongs to avenge. Sir Nicholas Maltby had just crushed out, with the most pitiless cruelty, a rising of the Bourkes of Connaught.

Sir Francis Crosby, the Queen's representative in Leix and Offaly, had conceived and executed the idea of preventing any further possible rising of the chiefs in those districts by summoning them and their kinsmen to a great banquet in the fort of Mullaghmast, and there massacring them all. Out of four hundred guests, only one man, a Lalor, escaped from that feast of blood. Of the clan O'Moore no less than one hundred and eighty chief men were slaughtered. One of the Moores had not come to that fatal banquet. Ruari Oge O'Moore, better known as 'Rory O'Moore,' devoted himself to avenging his murdered kinsmen, and the cry of 'Remember Mullaghmast!' sounded dismally in the ears of the settlers of King's and Queen's Counties for many a long year after, whenever Rory O'Moore made one of his swoops upon them with that shout for his battle-cry. With such memories in their minds, the tribes rose in all directions to the Desmond call. Early in the rising Fitzmaurice was killed in a scuffle. This was a heavy blow to the rebels; so was a defeat of the Geraldines by Sir Nicholas Maltby at Monaster. Elizabeth sent over more troops to Ireland under the new Lord Deputy, Sir William Pelham, who had with him as ally Ormonde, the head of the house of Butler, hereditary foes of the Geraldines, and easily induced to act against them. Pelham and Ormonde cut their way over Munster, reducing the province by unexampled ferocity. Ormonde boasted that he had put to death nearly six thousand disaffected persons. Just at this moment some of the Chiefs of the Pale rose, and rose too late. They gained one victory over Lord Grey de Wilton in the pass of Glenmalure, where the troops were completely routed by the Chief of Glenmalure, Feach M'Hugh, whom the English called 'the Firebrand of the Mountains.' Grey immediately abandoned the Pale to the insurgents, and turned to Smerwick, where some eight hundred Spanish and Italian soldiers had just landed too late to be of any service to the rebellion, and had occupied the dismantled fort. It was at once blockaded by sea and by land. In Grey's army Sir Walter Raleigh and Edmund Spenser both held commands. Smerwick, surrendered at discretion, and the prisoners were killed by Raleigh and his men in cold blood. Flushed by this success, Grey returned to the Pale and carried all before him. The Geraldines were disheartened, and were defeated wherever they made a stand. Lord Kildare was arrested on suspicion of treason, and sent to London to die in the Tower. Martial law was proclaimed in Dublin, and everyone, gentle or simple, suspected of disaffection was promptly hanged. Munster was pacified by an unstinted use of sword and gallows. The Desmond held out for a time, but he was caught at last and killed in the Slievemish Mountains, and his head sent to London to adorn the Tower. Munster was so vigorously laid waste that Mr. Froude declares that 'the lowing of a cow or the sound of a ploughboy's whistle was not to be heard from Valentia to the Rock of Cashel.'

Holinshed declares the traveller would not meet any man, woman, or child, saving in towns or cities, and would not see any beast; and Spenser gives a melancholy picture of the misery of the inhabitants, 'as that any stony heart would rue the same.' They were driven by misery to eat dead bodies scraped out of the grave; and Sir William Pelham proudly tells the queen how he has reduced the inhabitants to prefer being slaughtered to dying of starvation. Being thus pacified, Munster was now divided into seigniories of from 4,000 to 12,000 acres, to be held in fee of the crown at a quit rent of from 2d. to 3d. per acre, by such adventurers as cared to struggle with the dispossessed Irish.

The next step was to confiscate the estates of the rebellious chieftains. Sir John Perrot succeeded Lord Grey as deputy. He summoned a Parliament at which many of the Irish chiefs, persuaded, no doubt, by the strength of England's recent arguments, attended in English dress. The Parliament was perfectly manageable. It attainted anyone whom the Lord Deputy wished attainted. The estates of Desmond and some hundred and forty of his followers came to the Crown. The land was then distributed at the cheapest rate in large tracts to English nobles and gentlemen adven turers, who were pledged to colonize it with English labourers and tradesmen. But of these labourers and tradesmen not many came over, and those who did soon returned, tired of struggling for their foothold with the dispossessed Irish. In default of other tenants, the new owners of the soil were practically forced to take on the natives as tenants at will, and thus the desired change of population was not effected.

Perrot was a stern but not a merciless man, with a fierce temper, which made him many enemies among his own colleagues. He disliked the policy of Bingham in Connaught, and challenged him. He had a difference of opinion with Sir Henry Bagnal, and thought he had settled it when he had knocked Bagnal down. Nor was he more popular with the Irish. He treacherously captured Hugh Roe, or Red Hugh O'Donnell, son of Hugh O'Donnell, Tyrconnel, and kept him in Dublin Castle as a hostage for his father's good behaviour, and thus made young Red Hugh a bitter and dangerous enemy to the Crown. In the end Perrot was recalled and Sir William Fitzwilliam sent in his stead.

After six years of an exasperating rule, Fitzwilliam gave place in 1594 to Sir William Russell, who found the country hopelessly disorganized. Red Hugh had escaped from Dublin Castle to his Sept in Donegal, and his father had resigned the chieftainship to him. The dragoonings of Sir Richard Bingham had driven Connaught to desperation. The northern tribes were disturbed; some were in rebellion. Ulster, which had kept quiet all through the Desmond rebellion, was stirred by the spirit of sedition, and its great chief, Hugh O'Neil of Tyrone, was thought to be discontented and dangerous.

Hugh O'Neil, the grandson of that Con O'Neil whom Henry VIII. had made Earl of Tyrone, had been brought up at the English court, and confirmed in the lordship of Tyrone by the English Government. In the brilliant court of Elizabeth the young Irish chief was distinguished for his gifts of mind and body. When he came of age he was allowed to return to Ireland to his earldom. Once within his own country he assumed his ancestral title of The O'Neil, and revived all the

customs of independent Irish chieftains, For long
enough he took no part in any plots or movements
against the Crown; but many things, the ties of friendship and of love, combined to drive him into rebellion.
He had been deeply angered by the imprisonment of
his kinsman, Red Hugh, and when Red Hugh escaped,
burning with a sense of his wrongs and a desire for revenge, he brought all his influence to bear upon O'Neil
to draw him into a confederation against the Government. Another and more romantic cause helped to
drive Tyrone into revolt. After the death of his first
wife he had fallen in love with the beautiful sister of
Sir Henry Bagnal, the Lord Marshal, and the lady had
returned his love. In defiance of the fierce opposition
of her brother, she eloped with the Irish chief, and made
Bagnal the remorseless enemy of Tyrone.

Bagnal used all his influence to discredit Tyrone in
the eyes of the English Government, and he succeeded.
Urged by Red Hugh and the rebellious chiefs on the
one side, and by the enmity of Bagnal and the growing
distrust of the English Government on the other, Tyrone in the end consented to give the powerful support
of his name and his arms to a skilfully planned confederation of the tribes. On all sides the Irish chiefs
entered into the insurrection. O'Neil was certainly the
most formidable Irish leader the English had yet en-
countered. He was a brilliant general and a skilled
politician, and even Mr. Froude admits that ' his career
is unstained with personal crimes.' He defeated an
English army under Bagnal at the Blackwater, after a
fierce battle, inflamed by more than mere national ani-
mosity. Each leader was animated by a bitter hatred
of his opponent, which lends something of an Homeric
character to the struggle by the Blackwater. But Tyrone was fortunate in war as in love. Bagnal's forces
were completely defeated, and Bagnal himself killed.
Fortune seemed to smile on Tyrone's arms. Victory
followed victory. In a little while all Ireland, with the
exception of Dublin and a few garrison towns, was in
the hands of the rebels. Essex, and the largest army
ever sent to Ireland, crossed the Channel to cope with

him; but Essex made no serious move, and after an interview with Tyrone, in which he promised more than he could perform, he returned to England to his death. His place was taken by Lord Mountjoy, who, for all his love of angling and of Elizabethan 'play-books,' was a stronger man. Tyrone met him, was defeated. From that hour the rebellion was over. A Spanish army that had come to aid the rebels hurriedly re-embarked; many of the chiefs began to surrender; wild Red Hugh O'Donnell, flying to Spain to rouse allies, was poisoned and died. The sufferings of the Irish were terrible. Moryson, Mountjoy's secretary, a great traveller for his time, a Ulysses of ten years' wanderings, tells much the same stories of the after-consequences of this revolution, which were told by Spenser of the former. The carcases of people lay in ditches, their dead mouths open, green with the docks and nettles on which they had endeavoured to support life. Young children were trapped and eaten by the starving women who were hiding in the woods on the Newry. He and Sir Arthur Chichester witnessed the horrible spectacle of three young children devouring the entrails of their dead mother.

At last Tyrone was compelled to come to terms. He surrendered his estates, renounced all claim to the title of The O'Neil, abjured alliance with all foreign powers, and promised to introduce English laws and customs into Tyrone. In return he received a free pardon and a re-grant of his title and lands by letters patent. Rory O'Donnell, Red Hugh's brother, also submitted, and was allowed to retain the title of Earl of Tyrconnel. Elizabeth was already dead, and the son of Mary Stuart was King of England when these terms were made; but they were not destined to do much good.

Tyrone was brought to London to meet King James. He stayed at Wanstead as Mountjoy's guest, where four-and-twenty years before he had been present at Leicester's entertainment of Queen Elizabeth. Those four-and-twenty years had brought many changes: they had carried away many gallant gentlemen and wise statesmen and brave soldiers; they had changed

Tyrone from the brilliant young man dreaming after liberty into the 'new man' of Elizabeth's successor.

Tyrone returned to Ireland, but not to peace. King James was determined to reform the country after his own fashion, and in King James's mind reform meant supporting the Protestant religion everywhere, enforcing all laws against the Catholics, crushing out whatever remains of the old Brehon laws still lingered in the country, and definitely establishing the English law, which only the English settlers liked, in its stead. Sir George Carew had been deputy, and had come back to England with a store of money, and Chichester was in his place making himself hateful to the Irish by his ingenious methods of wresting their land from its rightful owners, and by his pitiless intolerance of the Catholic religion. The Irish Catholics had hoped for toleration from James—James, indeed, promised them on his accession the privilege of exercising their religion in private; but he soon revoked his promise, and the state of the Irish Catholics was worse than before. Tyrconnel himself was called upon to conform to the English faith. Lest these and kindred exasperations might arouse once more the dangerous wrath of the chiefs, Chichester enforced a rigorous disarmament of the Kernes. It is hardly to be wondered at if the reforming spirit of James did not greatly commend itself to two such national leaders as Tyrone and Tyrconnel; it would not be very surprising if they had thoughts of striving against it. Whether they had such thoughts or not, they were accused of entertaining them. They were seen to be dangerous enemies to the king's policy, whom it would be convenient to have out of the way, and they were proclaimed as traitors. They seem to have been convinced of the impossibility of resistance just then; they saw that it was death to remain, and they fled into exile. 'It is certain,' says the Four Masters, 'that the sea never carried, and the winds never wafted, from the Irish shores individuals more illustrious or noble in genealogy, or more renowned for deeds of valour, prowess, and high achievements.' Tyrone with his wife, Tyrconnel with his sister and friends and followers, ninety-nine in all, set sail in one smal boat on the 14th September, 1607, and tossed for twenty-one days upon the raging waves of the sea. We hear of O'Neil trailing his golden crucifix at the vessel's wake to bring about a calm; of two storm-worn merlins who took shelter in the rigging and were kindly cared for by the Irish ladies. On the 4th of October they landed at Quillebœuf, on the coast of France, and made their way to Rouen, receiving kind treatment at all hands. James demanded their surrender, but Henri Quatre refused to comply, though he advised the exiles to go into Flanders.

Into Flanders they went, their ladies giving the Marshal of Normandy those two storm-worn merlins they had cherished as a token of their gratitude for his kindness. From Flanders, in time, they made their way to Rome, and there they lived in exile, and died long years after. Tyrconnel died first, in 1608, and the Four Masters weep over his early eclipse. Clad in the simple robe of a Franciscan friar, he was buried in the Franciscan church of St. Pietro in Montorio, where the Janiculum over looks the glory of Rome, the yellow Tiber and the Alban Hills, the deathless Coliseum and the stretching Campagna. Raphael had painted his transfiguration for the grand altar; the hand of Sebastiano del Piombo had coloured its walls with the scourging of the Redeemer. Close at hand tradition marks the spot where Peter was crucified. In such a spot, made sacred by all that art and religion could lend of sanctity, the spirit of Tyrconnel rested in peace at last. His companion in arms and in misfortune survived him some eight years. We have a melancholy picture of old Tyrone wandering about in Rome, and wishing in vain to be back in his own land and able to strike a good blow for her. He died at last on July 20th, 1616, in the seventy-sixth year of his age, a brave, sad, blind old man. He was buried in the little church on the Janiculum, by the side of Tyrconnel.

CHAPTER V.

THE CROMWELLIAN SETTLEMENT.

AFTER the flight of the earls, Ireland was entirely in James's hands. The very few who opposed his authority were sternly and summarily dealt with. His writ ran in every part of the island; there was a sheriff for every shire; the old Irish law was everywhere superseded; there was nothing to interfere with James's schemes for confiscating Irish land and planting Irish provinces. The English had already made strong settlements in Leinster, Connaught, and Munster. Ulster had hitherto been practically untouched, but now at last it too was to come under the control of the Crown. The alleged treason of the two earls served as an excuse for confiscating the counties of Donegal, Derry, Tyrone, Fermanagh, Cavan, and Armagh. A sort of commission sat at Limavaddy to parcel out the lands of men who had committed no other offence than that of serving under the exiled chieftains. Ulster was planted with a thoroughly Protestant and anti-Irish colony of English and Scotch adventurers, and the Irish were driven away from the fertile lands like Red Indians to contracted and miserable reservations, while the fighting-men were shipped off to swell the armies of Gustavus Adolphus. Twelve City of London companies bought great tracts of land in Derry at very cheap rates. Six of these companies—the Mercers, Salters, Skinners, Ironmongers, Fishmongers, and Drapers—still retain much of the property thus acquired. The disinheriting process was carried on not by force alone, but by fraud. Men called 'discoverers' made it their business to spy out flaws in titles of land, in order that they might be confiscated by the Crown.

Conspicuous among the English adventurers, a very mirror of the merits of his kind, is Richard Boyle, who afterwards became the first Earl of Cork. He was a man of very low beginnings. He has been happily described as a forger, a horse-thief, and a conniver at murder, who made Providence his inheritance and prospered by it. Boyle landed in Dublin on Midsummer Eve, June 23, 1588, with some twenty-seven pounds in his pocket, a couple of suits of clothes, a diamond ring and a gold bracelet, and of course his rapier and dagger. After seven years' stay, the adventurer was lucky enough, aided perhaps by the diamond ring and the gold bracelet, to win the heart and hand of a lady of Limerick with five hundred pounds a year. This was the beginning of his fortunes. From that hour lands and money accumulated about him. As long as he got it he little cared how it came. No man was more ready to lay his hands upon any property of the Church or otherwise that he could securely close them over. He swindled Sir Walter Raleigh, then in prison and near his death, out of his Irish land for a sum shamelessly below its value, and throve upon the swindle. He is a fair type of the men with whom James planted Ulster and Leinster, and with whom he would have planted Connaught, but that he died before he was able to carry that scheme into effect. But Charles inherited the scheme. Ingenious court lawyers investigated and invalidated the titles of the Connaught landlords, and Charles soon found himself the owner of all Connaught, in the same sense that a burglar is the owner of the watches, the plate, and jewels, that are the results of a successful 'plant.' But land was not enough for Charles; he wanted money He was always wanting money, and he found a means of raising it in Ireland by promising grants of civil and religious liberty to the Catholics in exchange for so much down. The money was soon forthcoming, but the promised liberties never came. Charles's great ally in the management of Ireland was Thomas Wentworth, to whom the government of the country was given. Strafford devoted the great abilities, of which Lord Digby truly said 'that God had given him the use and the devil the application,' to supporting Charles's fraudulent schemes' for extorting money, until his malign influence was removed by the summons to England which ended in his death. But when the revolution began in England which ended with the fall of the king's head, many of the Irish thought their time had come. In 1641 the remnant of native Irish in Ulster rose, under Sir Phelim O'Neil, against the oppression of the Scotch settlers. This rising of 1641 has been written about often enough by English historians, as if it were an act of unparalleled wickedness and ferocity. It is written of with horror and hatred as the 'massacre of 1641.' Mr. Froude in especial has lent all the weight of his name and his eloquence to this theory of a gigantic and well-organized massacre; but Mr. Froude's statements are too curiously in advance of his evidence, and his evidence too untrustworthy to claim much historical importance. The business of 1641 was bad enough without Mr. Froude doing his best to make it worse. In one part of Ireland a certain body of men for a short time rose in successful insurrection, and they killed their oppressors as their oppressors had always killed their kin, wherever they could get at them. Undoubtedly there were a great many people killed. That, of course, no one attempts, no one desires, to justify; but is must be remembered that it was no worse than any one of the many massacres of the Irish by the English, which had taken place again and again, any time within the memory of the men then living, to go no farther back. Far be it from me, far be it from anyone, to defend the cruelties that accompanied the rising of 1641; but it is only fair to remember that most nations that have been treated cruelly are cruel in their revenge when they get it, and the followers of Sir Phelim O'Neil believed they had as bitter wrongs to avenge as men can have. They had been taught lessons of massacre by their masters, and this was their first essay. The massacre of Mullaghmast, Essex's treacherous massacre of the clan O'Neil, the dragooning of Connaught by Bingham, the desolation of Munster, all these atrocities are slurred over in order to lend an uncontrasted horror to Irish crimes.

Mr. Prendergast and Mr. John Mitchel have both written to show the terrible exaggerations that have attended upon all representations of the rising of 1641. These are Irish historians; but an English historian, Mr. Goldwin Smith, is fairer than Mr. Froude. To him the early part of the rising presents a 'picture of the vengeance which a people, brutalized by oppression, wreaks in the moment of its brief triumph on its oppressor.' He considers it 'to have been unpremeditated, and opposed to the policy of the leaders;' and when the struggle had begun, 'the English and Scotch settlers perhaps exceeded the Irish in atrocity, especially when we consider their comparative civilization. The Irish population of Island Magee, though innocent of the rebellion, were massacred, man, woman, and child, by the Scotch garrison of Carrickfergus.' The historian Borlase, kinsman to the chief justice of that name, rejoicing over the exploit of the soldiers against the rebels, mentions as one item how Sir W. Cole's regiment 'starved and famished of the vulgar sort, whose goods were seized on by this regiment, 7,000.' No cruelties on the one side can ever justify retaliation on the other, but to mention them will at least serve to dispel the idea which Mr. Froude would willingly foster, that at a sudden point in the history of a blameless and bloodless rule, some wicked Irish rose up and slew some of their just and merciful masters. The masters were neither just nor merciful, bloodless nor blameless. It was hardly to be expected that a people, treated as they had been, would act very mercifully when their turn came. Yet in many cases they did act mercifully. The followers of Sir Phelim spared some lives they might have taken; pitied some who were in their power. There has been monstrous exaggeration about the stories of wholesale massacre. Most of the evidence given before the commission sent to inquire into the thing is given on hearsay, and it is on this evidence that the accounts of the massacre depend. Old women who were ill in bed, and saw nothing of the struggle, gave as evidence the statements of friends, who told them that in many places thousands of persons were massacred. Others, again, were assured of such slaughterings of hundreds and thousands of persons in different parts of the country by the rebels themselves, who display throughout the evidence a most remarkable taste for self-accusation. Equally valuable and veracious evidence testifies that the ghosts of the murdered were seen stalking abroad—that in the river near Portadown, where the worst of the killing was said to have been, the body of a man stood erect for three days in the middle of the water, and that corpses floated against the stream several days after they had been drowned, in order to meet one of their murderers who was crossing the bridge!

However it began, Sir Phelim O'Neil's rising soon flamed up into a general rebellion. One of the most prominent of its leaders was Roger Moore, the last of a stately, ruined family, one of whose ancestors had died in the Tower under Edward VI. He was a brave and honourable gentleman, whose handsome face and graceful bearing commended him closely to the men from whom he sought help, whom his eloquence was well calculated to persuade, and his statesmanlike prudence and foresight to encourage. His daring and gallantry endeared him to his followers, who were always ready to fight their best for the war cry of 'For God, our Lady, and Roger Moore.' At his instance Colonel Owen O'Neil, better known as Owen Roe, came over from Spain to consolidate and command the insurrection. He was a nephew of the great Tyrone who had died in Rome; he was a brave and gallant gentleman, of high and honourable position in the Spanish army; he was the natural leader of the Irish people. Success at first was strewn before his feet. A National Convention met at Kilkenny in October, 1642, to establish the independence of Ireland. It took upon itself all the powers of a Provisional Government: appointed the officers of its army; organized provincial councils; issued proclamations; ordered its own seal to be cut; established a mint for coining its own money, and in every way showed itself ready to carry out the work of national administration. Frequent help came from abroad. In O'Neil's hands the army acquired new strength, and the struggle was carried on with marked humanity. The insurrection seemed in a fair way to become a successful revolution. There were altogether four parties in Ireland, three of whom it was to the king's advantage to conciliate. The fourth and least important was that of the Puritans and the English Parliament, headed by the Lord Justices Parsons and Borlase, whom Mr. Goldwin Smith describes as a pair of scoundrels who had done their best to foment the rebellion for their own advantage, and Generals Munroe and Coote the cruel. The three other parties were, first, the native Irish, under Owen Roe, guided by the Papal Nuncio Rinuccini, who had come over from Rome to lend his support and counsels to the movement; second, the Anglo-Irish, chiefly composed of Catholic nobles, who supported the king but stood out for their own rights and religion; and, thirdly, the king's party, with his Lord-Deputy, Lord Ormond, at its head. Lord Ormond was a Protestant, entirely devoted to his king, and compelled to play a very difficult game in trying to keep together the rebellious Irish who were willing to support Charles, and yet at the same time avoid giving offence to Charles's English followers, who wished for no terms with the Irish. Like most of the Irish leaders of his time, Ormond had had a strangely chequered career. He was the grandson of the eleventh Earl of Ormond, whose estates had been unjustly filched from him by his son-in-law, Sir Richard Preston, who had obtained the favour of James, and with it the patent of the earldom of Desmond. Young James Butler seemed thus quite cut off from his inheritance, but he was lucky enough to meet and win the affections of Preston's daughter, his cousin. He married her, and so in time came into not only the title of Earl of Ormond, but into the possession of the good broad lands of the family. Ormond had managed his own affairs skilfully enough, but he was not the man to fill a position of great and responsible statesmanship. His mediocre abilities and temporizing spirit were quite unsuited to the desperate circumstances in which he was placed.

Charles himself, harassed by English revolutionists at home, made many and any pledges to the Irish revolutionists, in the hope of winning them to his side. He never had the chance of breaking these pledges. The execution at Whitehall left Cromwell free to deal with Ireland. He entered Ireland with 8,000 foot and 4,000 horse, and marched from victory to victory. Everything was in his favour: his own military genius, the laurels of Worcester and Naseby, the disorganization of the Irish parties and the contentions that had sprung up amongst them, especially the removal of the only man really capable of doing anything against the Lord General in the field. Owen Roe O'Neil died suddenly, it was said, of course, by poison, though there seems little reason to believe this, and with his death all chance of the independence dreamed of by the Kilkenny Convention was over for that time. Roger Moore, the gallant and heroic, was already dead, killed, it was said, by bitter disappointment at the gradual failure of the cause he had so much at heart. Sir Phelim O'Neil was captured soon after. However he had lived, he died like a brave man; he was offered a pardon if he would only say that he took up arms by the king's command, but he preferred to die. One after another the Irish leaders surrendered or were defeated. The king's party was practically nowhere. Ormond had fled to France for his life. After Cromwell had captured Drogheda and put all its people to the sword; after he had conquered Wexford and slaughtered no less pitilessly its inhabitants, the revolution was at an end. Ireland was at Cromwell's mercy, and like all his predecessors, he resolved to make a new settlement.

The government of Ireland was now vested in a deputy commander-in-chief and four commissioners, with a high court of justice, which dealt out death, exile, and slavery in liberal measure. The Parliament had soothed the claims of its army by giving its officers and men debentures for Irish land, and similar debentures were held by a vast number of adventurers, who had speculated thus in Irish land, while the struggle was going on, to the amount of some 2,500,000 acres.

These claims had now to be settled; but the adventurers were not willing to settle until all possible danger was removed. There were disbanded soldiers in Ireland who might interfere with the peaceful settlements of Cromwellian would-be landlords, and these must be got rid of before any serious plantation could be effected. Word was sent throughout Europe that nations friendly to the Commonwealth would not beat their drums in vain in the market places of Irish garrison towns. The valour of Irish soldiers was well enough known abroad. It had been praised by William the Silent and Henry Quatre, and the redeemer of Holland and the victor of Ivry were good judges of tall soldiers. So the drums of Spain, Poland, and France were set rattling all over Ireland, and to their tuck the disbanded soldiery marched away to the number of 44,000, between 1651 and 1654, to die beneath foreign banners on foreign fields. Women and girls who were in the way of the adventurers could be got rid of no less profitably to West Indian planters weary of maroon and negro women. Into such shameful slavery thousands of unhappy Irishwomen were sent, and it was only when, the Irish supply being exhausted, the dealers in human flesh began to seize upon English women to swell their lists, that the practice was prohibited. Sir William Petty states that 6,000 boys and girls were sent to the West Indies, and the total number transported there and to Virginia was estimated at 10,000. Henry Cromwell not only approved of the exportation by force of some thousand 'Irish wenches' for the consolation of the soldiers in the newly-acquired colony of Jamaica, but of his own motion suggested the shipment also of from 1,500 to 2,000 boys of from twelve to fourteen years of age. 'We could well spare them,' he says, 'and who knows but it might be a means to make them English —I mean Christians?'

Now came the turn of the adventurers. The Government reserved for themselves all the towns, Church land, and tithes, and the counties Kildare, Dublin, Carlow, and Cork, to satisfy friends and favourites who were not army men. The portion of each adventurer in Ulster, Leinster, or Munster, was decided by lot, at a lottery held in Grocers' Hall, London, in July, 1653. To make the condition of the adventurers comfortable, each of the planted counties was divided in half, and the adventurers were quartered for their greater encouragement and protection in alternate baronies with soldier settlers. The rest of Ireland, except Connaught, was apportioned to satisfy the arrears of officers and soldiers. To keep the new settlers free from all Irish influences, Connaught was appointed as a reservation for the Irish, and all English holding lands in Connaught were allowed to exchange them for estates of equal value in other parts of Ireland. The Irish were then driven and cooped into Connaught. They were not allowed to appear within two miles of the river or four miles of the sea, and a rigorous passport system was established, to evade which was death without form of trial. Irish noblemen who were pardoned for being Irish were compelled to wear a distinctive mark upon their dress under pain of death, and persons of inferior rank bore a black spot on the right cheek, under pain of branding or the gallows. It is curious to reflect that all these precautions were not able to secure the Ironsides from the dreaded Irish influence, and that forty years later many of the children of Cromwell's troopers could not speak a word of English.

The plantation of the unhappy Irish in Connaught was slowly and sternly accomplished. Landowners had the choice of becoming the tenants at will of the new settlers, or of dying on the road side. The commissioners were much harassed in the execution of their task by the unreasonable clamour of the dispossessed Irish, who objected to being reserved in Connaught, and complained that the whole of the province was waste from famine. There were parts of Connaught where it was truly said that there was not wood enough to hang, water enough to drown, or earth enough to bury a man. The commissioners, anxious, no doubt, that the Irish should know the worst at once, had sent the earliest transplanted to this inhospitable place, and their dismay communicated itself to the as yet untransplanted. The hunted and harassed Irish nobles would not transplant themselves. It needed some punishments by death to quicken the general desire to seek the appointed haven west of the Shannon. But death not proving convenient, as executions would have had to be ordered wholesale, it was decided to ship off the restive Irish who would not go to Connaught to the West Indies. But the unhappy wretches who got to Connaught were not at the end of their misery. The officers employed to settle them in their new homes had to be bribed by money or by portion of the reserved land to carry out the law, and the greedy officers were easily able to force the unhappy transplanters to sell the rest of their reduced lots at miserably small rates. The transplanted, rich and poor, were wretchedly lodged in smoky cabins or under the open air, and lay down and measured out their graves in common confusion and misery, peer with peasant, starved to death.

The towns were cleared as well. The inhabitants of Limerick, Galway, Waterford, and Wexford, were ejected with scant compensation and scanter ceremony to make room for English merchants from Liverpool and Gloucester. The dispossessed Irish merchants fled across the seas to carry their skill and thrift to other lands, and in the new hands the commercial prosperity of the towns dwindled away. Galway, that had been a flourishing sea-port, never recovered her resettlement. The Irish who were dispossessed, and who would not transplant or go into exile, took to the woods and mountains, the clefts of the rocks and the caves of the earth, and lived a life of wild brigandage, like the Greek Klephts dispossessed by the Turk. The Government put a price upon the heads alike of these Tories, of priests, and of wolves.

CHAPTER VI.

THE RESTORATION.—WILLIAM OF ORANGE.

WHEN Cromwell and the Cromwellian rule had passed away and the Stuart king came over to 'enjoy his own again,' most of the dispossessed Irish gentlemen, whose loyalty to his cause and creed had cost them their estates, and driven them to exile abroad, or worse than exile, in the Connaught reservations, thought not unreasonably that they might be allowed to 'enjoy their own again,' too, as well as their merry monarch. They were grievously disappointed. The Cromwellian landholders were quite prepared to secure their estates by loyal recognition of the new rule, and their adhesion was far more serviceable to the Second Charles than the allegiance of the ruined Irish gentlemen. Men like Broghill were not prepared to let the lands they had got during the Cromwellian settlement slip between their fingers. Broghill, the infamous Broghill, as he has been justly called, was a worthy son of the adventurer Richard Boyle, who has passed into history as the 'great Earl of Cork.' Boyle was a great robber, but Broghill was a greater, and a traitor as well. He had served every ruling Government in turn, and had always contrived to make his subservience profitable to himself. He got into the good graces of Cromwell by the signal services he rendered to his cause in Ireland, but he was not prepared to sacrifice the rewards of these services, the fair acres he had laid hold of, to any sentimental adherence to the Cromwellian principle. His treachery secured the Restoration as far as Ireland was concerned; he played Monk's part upon the Irish stage. The breath once out of Cromwell's body, he prepared to intrigue for the return of Charles. He found an able assistant in Coote, the cruel president of Connaught. Charles rewarded the faithful Broghill with the confirmation in all his estates, and the title of Earl of Orrery. Coote was confirmed in his estates and made Earl of Mountrath. This worthy pair of brothers were made Lords Justices of Ireland, and in their hands the settlement of the Land Question was practically left. It is easy to see that it was to the interest of neither that there should be a general redistribution of land. They arranged an ingenious scheme by which only those who proved themselves 'innocent' of a certain series of offences should be reinstated. No man was to be held 'innocent' who had not belonged to the Royal party before 1643, or who had been engaged in the Confederacy before 1648, or who had adhered to the party of the Papal Nuncio. Lest this might not sufficiently limit the list of the 'innocent,' it was decided that no one deriving his title from such offenders, and no one who played a merely passive part, living, that is to say, on his estate, and leaning neither to the one side nor the other, should be allowed to regain the lands he had lost. This system was so well worked that except in the rarest cases the plundered Irish were unable to get back an acre of land from the new men. Ormond and a few others were restored at once to their estates and honours without any difficulty, and the rest were left as they were.

Ormond was made Lord Lieutenant, and once again showed that he was not strong enough for his stormy times. He opposed, but could not prevent, the efforts of the English Cabal to prohibit the importation of Irish cattle as a nuisance. The Cabal found no difficulty in carrying their point; their only difficulty was whether they should describe the obnoxious importation as a 'detriment' or a 'nuisance,' a difficulty which Clarendon satirically proposed to meet by suggesting that it might as fittingly be called 'adultery.' When the cattle trade was put down, Ormond (he was now duke of that name) did his best to advance the Irish woollen and linen trades, but these efforts rendered him hateful to the Cabal, and he was removed from office. For long enough he lingered in disgrace, attending at Charles's court in London, and quietly enduring the insults that Charles and his favourites put upon him, and the dangers of assassination to which his enemies exposed him. At length he was restored to the Irish Lord Lieutenantship, and the record of his last administration is chiefly a record of measures against the Roman Catholics. Charles indeed was anxious to allow the Catholics as much toleration as possible, but the fury of the Titus Oates Plot found its echo across the Irish sea. Ormond's nature was not one which lent itself to excesses of any kind, but he was strongly anti-Catholic, and to him is due the dishonour of sending Plunkett, the Archbishop of Armagh, to his trial and death in England, a 'murder' which, as Mr. Goldwin Smith says, 'has left a deep stain on the ermine of English justice.'

With James's accession the treatment of the Catholics changed considerably. Ormond was recalled to end his days in peaceful retirement, and his place was taken by a new and remarkable figure, the bearer of a historic name. This new man was James Talbot, Earl of Tyrconnel. He was, while a boy, in Drogheda during the Cromwellian sack, and the memory of that fearful hour was always with him. He had followed the Stuarts into exile; he was the first Roman Catholic Governor of Ireland appointed since the introduction of the Protestant religion. He did his best to undo the severe anti-Catholic legislation which marked Ormond's last administration. That he, a Catholic and an Irishman, should wish to see justice and religious liberty allowed to his countrymen and the companions of his faith has made his name too often the object of the obloquy and the scorn of historians who are unwilling to see liberty, either political or religious, enjoyed by any but themselves and their own people or party. The war between James and William of Orange found the Catholics in Ireland entirely on the Stuart side, though more for the sake of Talbot of Tyrconnel than of the English monarch. Talbot might have said of himself, like Shakespeare's English Talbot, that he was 'but shadow of himself,' and that 'his substance, sinews, arms, and strength' lay in the Irish Catholics who rallied round him as they had before rallied round an earlier wearer of the name of Tyrconnel. For a time it seemed as if this Irish support might shoulder James into his throne again, and the King made many concessions to encourage such allegiance. Poynings's Act was formally repealed, and a measure passed restoring the dispossessed Irish to their property. A large army came over from France to Ireland to fight for the Stuart, under the command of one of the bravest and vainest soldiers that ever fought a field, St. Ruth. But the battle of the Boyne ruined alike the Stuart cause and the hopes of its Irish adherents. Ginckel, William's ablest general, took Athlone, defeated the French and Irish at Aughrim, where the glorious and vain-glorious St. Ruth was slain, and invested Limerick. In Limerick Tyrconnel died, and at Limerick the last struggle was made. The city was held by Patrick Sarsfield, a brave Catholic gentleman and a gifted soldier. He defended Limerick so well against hopeless odds that he was able to wring from his enemies a treaty providing that the Roman Catholics of Ireland should enjoy the privilege of religious freedom, and giving King James's followers the right of their estates. When the treaty was signed, Sarsfield surrendered the city and marched out with all the honours of war. Outside of the city the flags of England and France were set up, and the defenders of Limerick were offered their choice of service under either standard. Ginckel had the mortification of seeing the flower of the army rally beneath the lilies of Gaul, only a few regiments ranging themselves beneath the English standard. These Irish soldiers did splendid service in the land to which they gave their swords. Their names became famous in France, in Spain, in Austria, and in Russia, and on many a field from Fontenoy to Ramilies and Laufeldt the Irish brigades fought out for an alien cause, and beneath a foreign flag, the old quarrel of their race. Sarsfield himself died bravely at Landen, three years after the surrender of Limerick. It is said that the dying man looked at his hand, red with his own blood, and said, 'Would God that this were shed for Ireland.' All that he had done for his country had been done in vain. The treaty that he had secured by his gallant defence of Limerick, the treaty that had been confirmed and even amplified by William himself, was broken and set aside. Mr. Froude seems to think that the Irish ought to have been aware that the English could not be expected to keep faith with them over such a treaty. To such sorry justification for such a breach of faith there is nothing to say. The treason shows worse when it is remembered that after the treaty was signed an army of reinforcements arrived in the Shannon. Had these come some days earlier, the siege of Limerick must inevitably have been raised. Even as it was Ginckel greatly feared that Sarsfield might seize the opportunity to renew the war. But Sarsfield honourably abided by his word. The treaty was violated; all the forfeited lands were reconfiscated and sold by auction as before, for the benefit of the State, to English corporations and Dublin merchants. At William's death the Catholics were the owners of less than one seventh of the whole area of Ireland. William determined to make Ireland Protestant by Penal Laws. Under these laws Catholics could not sit in the Irish Parliament, or vote members to it. They were excluded from the army and navy, the corporations, the magistracy, the bar, the bench, the grand juries, and the vestries. They could not be sheriffs or soldiers, game-keepers or constables. They were forbidden to own any arms, and any two justices or sheriffs might at any time issue a search warrant for arms. The discovery of any kind of weapon rendered its Catholic owner liable to fines, imprisonment, whipping, or the pillory. They could not own a horse worth more than five pounds, and any Protestant tendering that sum could compel his Catholic neighbour to sell his steed. No education whatever was allowed to Catholics. A Catholic could not go to the university; he might not be the guardian of a child; he might not keep a school, or send his children to be educated abroad, or teach himself. No Catholic might buy land, or inherit, or receive it as a gift from Protestants, or hold life annuities or leases for more than thirty-one years, or any lease on such terms as that the profits of the land exceeded one third the value of the land. If a Catholic purchased an estate, the first Protestant who informed against him became its proprietor. The eldest son of a Catholic, upon apostatising, became heir at law to the whole estate of his father, and reduced his father to the position of a mere life tenant. A wife who apostatised was immediately freed from her husband's control, and assigned a certain proportion of her husband's property. Any child, however young, who professed to be a Protestant, was at once taken from his father's care, and a certain proportion of his father's property assigned to him. In fact, the Catholics were excluded, in their own country, from every profession, from every Government office from the highest to the lowest, and from almost every duty or privilege of a citizen. It was laid down from the bench by Lord Chancellor Bowes and Chief Justice Robinson that 'the law does not suppose any such person to exist as an Irish Roman Catholic,' and proclaimed from the pulpit by Dopping, bishop of Meath, that Protestants were not bound to keep faith with Papists. We are reminded, as we read, of Judge Taney's famous decision in the American Dred Scott case, that a black man had no rights which a white man was bound to respect. Happily humanity and civilization are in the end too much for the Doppings and Taneys. It is hard for a more enlightened age to believe that such laws as these were ever passed, or being passed were ever practised. It was well said that the penal code could not have been practised in hell, or it would have overturned the kingdom of Beelzebub. But these laws, by which the child was taught to behave himself proudly against the ancient and the base against the honourable, were rigorously enforced in Ireland. The records of the House of Lords are full of the vain appeals of Catholic gentlemen against their dispossession by some claimant, perhaps an unworthy member of their family, perhaps a bitter enemy, and perhaps a hitherto unknown 'discoverer,' who had put on the guise of ostentatious Protestantism as a cloak for plunder. In often-quoted, often-to-be-quoted words, Burke, in later years, denounced the penal code for its 'vicious perfection.' 'For,' said he, 'I must do it justice: it was a complete system, full of coherence and consistency, well digested and well composed in all its parts. It was a machine of wise and elaborate contrivance, and as well fitted for the oppression, impoverishment, and degradation of a people, and the debasement in them of human nature itself, as ever proceeded from the perverted ingenuity of man.' It is encouraging to think that even under such laws the spirit of the people was not wholly annihilated. The country clung to its proscribed faith; the ministers of that faith braved shame and persecution and death in their unswerving allegiance to their scattered flocks. They fought bravely against the oppression which would have enforced ignorance and all its attendant evils upon an unhappy people. When no Catholic might open a school, the priests established what were known as hedge schools. By the roadside and on the hillside, in ditches and behind hedges, the children of the people cowered about their pastors, fearfully and eagerly striving to attain that knowledge which the harsh laws denied them. In one other instance the penal laws failed. They could take away the Catholic's land, his horse, his life; they could hang his priests and burn his place of worship; they could refuse him all education; they could deny him all rights before the law except the right to be robbed and hanged; but they could not compel him to change his faith, and they could not succeed in making every Protestant in Ireland a willing creature of the new code. By the code, any marriage between a Catholic and a Protestant was, by the fact of the husband and wife being of opposite faiths, null and void, without any process of law whatever. A man might leave his wife, or a woman her husband, after twenty years of marriage in such a case, and bring a legal bastardy on all their offspring. But for the sake of human honour, it is consolatory to remember that the instances in which this ever occurred were very rare. The law might sanction the basest treachery, but it was not able to make its subjects treacherous.

The evils of the penal code were further supplemented by the statutory destruction of Irish trade. Under Charles I. Stafford had done his best to ruin the Irish woollen manufacturers in order to benefit the English clothiers. Under Charles II. the importation of Irish cattle, or sheep, or swine, was prohibited. In 1663 Ireland was left out of the Act for the encouragement of trade, so that all the carrying trade in Irish-built ships with any part of his Majesty's dominions was prevented. But it was left to William to do the worst. In 1696 all direct trade from Ireland with the British colonies was forbidden, and a revival of the woollen trade was crushed out by an Act which prohibited the export of Irish wool or woollen goods, from any Irish port except Cork, Drogheda, Dublin, Kinsale, Waterford, and Youghal, to any port in the world except Milford, Chester, Liverpool, and certain ports in the Bristol Channel, under a penalty of £500 and the forfeiture of both ship and cargo.

CHAPTER VII.

THE EIGHTEENTH CENTURY.

It has been happily said that Ireland has no history during the greater part of the eighteenth century. What Burke called 'the ferocious legislation of Queen Anne' had done its work of humiliation to the full. For a hundred years the country was crushed into quiescent misery. Against the tyranny which made war at once upon their creed, their intellect, and their trade, the Irish had no strength to struggle; neither in 1715 nor in 1745 did the Irish Catholics raise a hand for the Pretenders. The evidence of Arthur Young shows how terribly the condition of the peasantry had sunk when he is able to state that 'Landlords of consequence have assured me that many of their cottars would think themselves honoured by having their wives and daughters sent for to the bed of their masters; a mark of slavery which proves the oppression under which such people must live.' To add to the wretchedness of the people, a terrible famine ravaged the country in 1741, the horrors of which almost rival, in ghastliness, those of the famine of 1847. Great numbers died; great numbers fled from the seemingly accursed country to recruit the armies of the Continent, and found death less dreadful on many well-fought fields, than in the shape of plague or famine in their own land. Such elements of degradation and despair naturally begot all sorts of secret societies amongst the peasantry from north to south. Whiteboys, Oak-boys, and Hearts of Steel banded against the land tyranny and held together for long enough in spite of the strenuous efforts of the Government to put them down. If the military force, said Lord Chesterfield, 'had killed half as many landlords as it had Whiteboys, it would have contributed more effectually to restore quiet; for the poor people in Ireland are worse used than negroes by their masters, and deputies of deputies.'

Bad as the condition of Ireland was, the English in Ireland proposed to make it worse by depriving it of what poor remains of legislative independence it still possessed. So early as 1703, a petition in favour of union with England, and the abolition of the Irish Parliament, was presented to Queen Anne; its prayer was rejected for the time, but the idea was working in the minds of those—and they were many—who wished to see Ireland stripped of all pretence at independence afforded by the existence of a separate Parliament, even though that Parliament were entirely Protestant. Seventeen years later, in the sixth year of George I., a vigorous blow was dealt at the independence of the Irish Parliament by an Act which not only deprived the Irish House of Lords of any appellate jurisdiction, but declared that the English Parliament had the right to make laws to bind the people of the kingdom of Ireland. The 'heads of a Bill' might indeed be brought in in either House. If agreed to, they were carried to the Viceroy, who gave them to his Privy Council to alter if they choose, and send to England. They were subject to alteration by the English Attorney-General, and when approved by the English Privy Council, sent back to Ireland, where the Irish Houses could either accept or reject them *in toto*, but had no power to change them.

The condition of the Irish Parliament all through the eighteenth century is truly pitiable. Its existence as a legislative body is a huge sham, a ghastly simulacrum. It slowly drifted into the custom of sitting but once in every two years to vote the Money Bills for the next two twelvemonths. The Irish Exchequer derived half its receipts from the Restoration grant of the Excise and Customs; and the greater part of this money was wasted upon royal mistresses, upon royal bastards, and upon royal nominees. The Parliament was torn by factions which the English Government ingeniously played off against each other; it was crowded with the supple placemen of the Government, who were well rewarded for their obedient votes; the bulk of the House was made up of nominees of the Protestant landlords. The Opposition could never turn out the Administration, for the Administration was composed of the irremovable and irresponsible Lords Justices of the Privy Council and certain officers of State. The Opposition, such as it was, was composed of Jacobites who dreamed of a Stuart Restoration, and of a few men animated by a patriotic belief in their country's rights. These men were imbued with the principles which had been set forth in the end of the seventeenth century by William Molyneux, the friend of Locke, who, in his 'Case of Ireland,' was the first to formulate Ireland's constitutional claim to independent existence. His book was burnt by the English Parliament, but the doctrines it set forth were not to be so destroyed. During the reigns of the first two Georges, the Patriot Party had the support of the gloomy genius and the fierce indignation of the man whose name is coupled with that of Molyneux in the opening sentences of Grattan's famous speech on the triumph of Irish independence. Swift, weary of English parties, full of melancholy memories of St. John and Harley and the scattered Tory chiefs, had come back to Ireland to try his fighting soul in the troublous confusion of Irish politics. It has been asserted over and over again that Swift had very little real love for the country of his birth. Whether he loved Ireland or no is little to the purpose, for he did her very sterling service. He was the first to exhort Ireland to use her own manufactures, and he was unsuccessfully prosecuted by the State for the pamphlet in which he gave this advice. When Wood received the authority of the English Parliament to deluge Ireland with copper money of his own making, it was Swift's 'Drapier's Letters' which made Wood and his friends the laughingstock of the world and averted the evil. In Swift's 'Modest Proposal,' we have the most valuable evidence of the misery of the country. He suggests, with savage earnestness, that the children of the Irish peasant should be reared for food; and urges that the best of these should be reserved for the landlords, who, as they had already devoured the substance of the people, had the best right to devour the flesh of their children.

Even as the most conspicuous supporter of the Irish interest during the first half of the century was the Dean of St. Patrick's, the two most remarkable supporters of the English 'interest' in Ireland in the eighteenth century were both Churchmen, the Primate Boulter and the Primate Stone. Compared to Stone, Boulter appears an honest and an honourable man. He was only shallow, arrogant, and capricious, quite incapable of the slightest sympathy with any people or party but his own—a man of some statesmanship, which was entirely at the service of the Government, and which never allowed him to make any consideration for the wants, the wishes, or the sufferings of the Irish people. Perhaps the best that can be said of him is, that while belonging to the English Church, he did not wholly neglect its teachings and its duties, or live a life in direct defiance of its commands, which is saying a good deal for such a man in such a time. So much cannot be said of his successor in the headship of the Irish ecclesiastical system, Primate Stone. The grandson of a gaoler, he might have deserved admiration for his rise if he had not carried with him into the high places of the Church a spirit stained by most of the crimes over which his ancestor was appointed warder. In an age of corrupt politics he was conspicuous as a corrupt politician; in a profligate epoch he was eminent for profligacy. In the basest days of the Roman Empire he would have been remarkable for the variety of his sins; and the grace of his person, which caused him to be styled in savage mockery the 'Beauty of Holiness,' coupled with his ingenuity in pandering to the passions of his friends, would have made him a serious rival to Petronius at the court of Nero.

The year that Swift died, 1745, was the first year of the Viceroyalty of Lord Chesterfield, one of the few bright spots in the dark account of Ireland in the eighteenth century. If all Viceroys had been as calm as reasonable, and as considerate as the author of the famous 'Letters' showed himself to be in his dealings with the people over whom he was placed, the history of the succeeding century and a half might have been very different. But when Chesterfield's Viceroyalty passed away, the temperate policy he pursued passed away as well, and has seldom been resumed by the long succession of Viceroys who have governed and misgoverned the country since.

In the meanwhile a new spirit was gradually coming over the country. Lucas, the first Irishman, in the words of the younger Grattan, 'who, after Swift, dared to write freedom,' had founded the *Freeman's Journal*, a journal which ventured in dangerous times to advocate the cause of the Irish people, and to defy the anger of the English 'interest.' In the first number, which appeared on Saturday, September 10, 1763, and which bore an engraving of Hibernia with a wreath in her right hand and a rod in her left, Lucas loudly advocated the duty and dignity of a free press, and denounced under the guise of 'Turkish Tyranny,' 'The Tyranny of French Despotism,' and 'The Ten Tyrants of Rome,' the ministries and the creature whom his unsparing eloquence assailed. The Patriot Party, too, was rapidly increasing its following and its influence in the country. The patriotic party in Parliament had found a brilliant leader in Henry Flood, a gifted politician, who thought himself a poet, and who was certainly an orator. Flood was the son of the Irish Chief Justice of the King's Bench. He had been educated at Trinity College and at Oxford, and much of his youth was devoted to the study of oratory and the pursuit of poetry. He wrote an ode to Fame, which was perhaps unlucky in reaching its address as that poem to posterity of which poor Jean Baptiste Rousseau was so proud. But his oratory was a genuine gift, which he carefully cultivated. We hear of his learning speeches of Cicero by heart, and writing out long passages of Demosthenes and Æschines. His character was kindly, sweet-tempered, and truthful. He was ambitious because he was a man of genius, but his ambition was for his country rather than for himself, and he served her with a daring spirit, which only the profound statesmanlike qualities of his intellect prevented from becoming reckless. In 1759, then in his twenty-seventh year, a married man with a large fortune, he entered public life, never to leave it till the end of his career. He came into Parliament as member for Kilkenny, and almost immediately became a prominent member of the Opposition. His maiden speech was a vigorous attack upon the corrupt and profligate Primate Stone. In the hands of Flood, ably seconded by Charles Lucas, the Opposition began to take shape, and to become a serious political power. Under his brilliant and skilful chieftainship, the 'Patriots,' as the party who followed him were called in scorn by their enemies, and in admiration by their allies, made repeated assaults upon the hated pension list. After they had been defeated again and again, Flood found a more successful means of harassing the Administration by turning the attention of his party to Parliamentary reform. The time was well chosen. The English Government was beginning to be troubled by its own greedy placemen, who were always ready to go with light hearts into the Opposition lobby if they could not squeeze all they wanted out of the Government. By taking advantage of the discontent of placemen, the patriots were able to induce the House to declare that they alone had the right to initiate a Money Bill, and to refuse to accept a Money Bill brought in by the English or Irish Privy Council. It is bitterly to be regretted that Flood allowed himself to be led away from the Patriot Party, and to accept a Government sinecure. There is no need to doubt that when Flood accepted the office of Vice-Treasurer he believed that he was acting on the whole in the interests of the cause he represented. He had just made a great political triumph. He had driven out of office a most obnoxious and unpopular Lord-Lieutenant, Lord Townsend, and Townsend's place had been taken by Lord Harcourt, a reasonable and able man, who seemed likely to be in sympathy with Flood's views as to the independence of Parliament. Flood may well be assumed to have reasoned that a place under Government would offer him greater opportunities for urging his cause. But, whatever his reasons, the step was fatally ill-advised; he lost the confidence of the country, and ruined his position as leader. But this was the less to be regretted that it gave his place as leader of the Patriot Party to a greater orator and a nobler man—to Henry Grattan.

Grattan was born in 1750, in Dublin. His years of early manhood were passed in London, studying for the Bar. Like Flood, he believed himself destined to be a poet; but when in 1775 he was nominated to represent Charlemont in the Irish Parliament by the owner of the borough, Lord Charlemont, he discovered where his real genius lay. He and Flood had been close friends and political allies until Flood's acceptance of the Vice-Treasurership. This seemed to Grattan the basest political apostacy. The alliance between the two orators was definitely broken off; the friendship was finally severed in the fierce discussion that took place between them in the House of Commons some years later, when Flood tauntingly described Grattan as a 'mendicant patriot,' and Grattan painted Flood as a traitor in one of the most crushing and pitiless pieces of invective that have ever belonged to oratory. Such a quarrel between such men was the more to be regretted because each had the same end in view, and each had special qualifications for furthering that end which were not possessed by the other.

Grattan was now leader of the Patriots. It was his ambition to secure legislative independence for the Irish Parliament. The war with the American colonies gave him the opportunity of realizing his ambition. A large force of volunteers had been organized in Ireland to defend the island from the attacks of the terrible Paul Jones, and the Volunteers and their leaders were all in sympathy with the Patriot Party. For the first time since the surrender of Limerick, there was an armed force in Ireland able and willing to sustain the national cause. There were 60,000 men under arms under the leadership of the gifted and patriotic Lord Charlemont. Among their leaders were Flood himself and Henry Grattan. The Volunteers formed themselves into an organized convention for the purpose of agitating the national grievances. Grattan was not indeed a member of this convention, but he saw that with the existence of the Volunteers had come the hour to declare the independence of the Irish Parliament, and he seized upon the opportunity. He had an army at his back; the English Government was still striving with Mr. Washington and his rebels, and it had to give way. All that Grattan asked for was granted; the hateful Sixth Act of George I. was repealed, and Grattan was able to address a free people and wish Ireland as a nation a perpetual existence.

But now that the desires of the Patriot Party had been apparently fulfilled, by a curious example of the law of historical reaction, the popularity of Grattan began to wane, and that of Flood to wax anew. The English hold over the Irish Parliament had been based first upon Poynings's Act, and then upon a Declaratory Act asserting the dependence of the Irish Parliament. It was this Declaratory Act that Grattan, aided by the Volunteers, had caused to be repealed, and he and his party contended that by this repeal England resigned her right over the Irish Parliament. Flood and his friends maintained that the repeal of the Declaratory Act was not enough, and they would not rest until they had obtained a fuller and more formal Renunciation Act. There were other differences between Flood and Grattan. Grattan was all in favour of the disbandment and dispersal of the Volunteers. Flood was for still keeping them in armed existence. Grattan had urged that their work had been done, and that their presence was a prætorian menace to the newly-acquired liberties. Flood believed that their co-operation was still needful for the further securing of Irish liberty. Yet it is curious to remember that Grattan was the advocate of Catholic Emancipation, and that Flood was strenuously opposed to it. Grattan carried his point, and the Volunteers disbanded and dispersed, very much to the disappointment of Flood and the indignation of one of the most curious political figures of the time, and one of the most remarkable of the many remarkable ecclesiastics who played a part in this period of Irish history. This was the Earl of Bristol and Bishop of Derry, a son of the Lord Hervey whom Pope strove to make eternally infamous by his nickname of Sporus, and who has left such living pictures of the court of the Second George in the brilliant malignancy of his unrivalled memoirs. The bishop was a cultured, desperate dandy, a combination of the typical French abbé of the last century with the conventional soldier of fortune. He loved gorgeous dresses; he loved to be prominent in all things. The Volunteers delighted his wild imagination. He fancied himself the leader of a great rebellion, and he babbled to everyone of his scheme with ostentátious folly. But though he could command popularity among the Volunteers, he could not command the Volunteers themselves. They remained under the guidance of Charlemont and Flood, and when Flood failed in carrying the Volunteer Reform Bill for enlarging the franchise, the Volunteers peaceably dissolved. The bishop drifted out of Dublin, drifted into Naples, lived a wild life there for many years, became a lover of Lady Hamilton's, and died in Rome in 1803.

While it lasted the free Irish Parliament was worthy of its creator. It gave the Catholics the elective franchise of which they had been so long deprived; up to this time no Catholic had been able to record a vote in favour of the men who were labouring for the liberty of their country. There is no doubt that it would in time have allowed Catholics to enter Parliament. But the efforts of Grattan after Catholic Emancipation failed, and their failure strengthened the hands of the United Irishmen.

The name 'United Irishmen,' designated a number of men all over the country who had formed themselves into clubs for the purpose of promoting a union of friendship between Irishmen of every religious persuasion, and of forwarding a full, fair, and adequate representation of all the people in Parliament. It was in the beginning a perfectly loyal body, with a Protestant gentleman, Mr. Hamilton Rowan, for its president.

James Napper Tandy, a Protestant Dublin trader, was secretary. The men who created it were well pleased with the success of Grattan's efforts at the independence of the Irish Parliament, but they were deeply discontented at the subsequent disbandment of the Volunteers and Grattan's comparative inaction. The simple repeal of the Sixth George did not answer their aspirations for liberty, which were encouraged and excited by the outbreak of the French Revolution. They found a leader in Theobald Wolfe Tone, a young barrister, brave, adventurous, and eloquent. Allied with him was Lord Edward Fitzgerald, the chivalrous, the heroic, who had lived long in France and travelled in America, who was devoted to two loves, his country and his beautiful wife Pamela, the daughter of Philippe Egalité and Madame de Genlis. A third leader was Arthur O'Connor, Lord Longueville's nephew, and member for Phillipstown. They were all young; they were all Protestants; they were all dazzled by the successes of the French Revolution, and believed that the House of Hanover might be as easily overturned in Ireland as the House of Capet had been in France. Wolfe Tone went over to Paris and pleaded the cause of Ireland with the heads of the French Directory. His eloquence convinced them, and a formidable fleet was sent over to Ireland under victorious Hoche. But the winds which had destroyed the Armada dispersed the French squadron, and no landing was effected. The Government was aroused and alarmed; the plans of the United Irishmen were betrayed; martial law was proclaimed. Arthur O'Connor was at once arrested. Edward Fitzgerald lay in hiding in Dublin for some days in a house in Thomas Street, but his hiding-place was betrayed. He defended himself desperately against the soldiers who came to take him, was severely wounded, and died of his wounds in prison. The room is still shown in which the 'gallant and seditious Geraldine' met his death; it is very small, and the struggle must have been doubly desperate in the narrow space. It is a dismal little theatre for the tragedy that was played in it.

Before the rebellion broke out, soldiers and yeomen, who were generally Orangemen of the most bitter kind, were sent to live at free quarters among the peasants in every place where any possible disaffection was suspected, and the licentiousness and brutal cruelty of these men did much to force hundreds of peasants into the rising, and to prompt the fierce retaliation which afterwards characterized some episodes of the rebellion. The troops and yeomen flogged, picketed, and tortured with pitch-caps the unhappy men, and violated the unhappy women, who were at their mercy. The Irish historian would indeed be fortunate who could write that on the Irish side the struggle was disgraced by no such crimes. Unhappily this cannot be said. Here it cannot be better than to speak in Mr. Lecky's words: 'Of the atrocities committed by the rebels during the bloody month when the rebellion was at its height, it is difficult to speak too strongly,' but he goes on to say— he is criticizing Mr. Froude—'an impartial historian would not have forgotten that they were perpetrated by undisciplined men, driven to madness by a long course of savage cruelties, and in most cases without the knowledge or approval of their leaders; that from the beginning of the struggle the yeomen rarely gave quarter to the rebels; that with the one horrible exception of Scullabogue the rebels in their treatment of women contrasted most favourably and most remarkably with the troops, and that one of the earliest episodes of the struggle was the butchery near Kildare of 350 insurgents who had surrendered on the express promise that their lives should be spared.

It should be borne in mind, in considering the rebellion of 1798, that the struggle is not to be considered as a struggle of creed against creed. Protestants began and organized the movement, and it is estimated by Madden that among the leaders of the United Irishmen, Catholics were only in the proportion of one to four throughout the rebellion. On the other hand, a large number of Catholics were strongly opposed to the rebellion, and in many cases took active measures against it. In Wexford, unhappily, the efforts of the

Orangemen succeeded in giving the struggle there much of the character of a religious war, but this the revolution looked at as a whole never was. It was a national movement, an uprising against intolerable grievances, and it was sympathized with and supported by Irishmen of all religious denominations, bound together by common injuries and a common desire to redress them.

The great insurrection which was to have shattered the power of England was converted into a series of untimely, abortive local risings, of which the most successful took place in Wexford. The rebels fought bravely, but the cause was now hopeless. The Catholic clergy came fearlessly to the front; many of the little bands of rebels were led into action by priests of the Church. Father John Murphy, Father Philip Roche, and Father Michael Murphy, were among the bravest and ablest of the revolutionary leaders. Father Michael Murphy was long believed by his men to be invulnerable, but he was killed by a cannon ball in the fight by Arklow. Father Philip Roche also died on the field. Father John Murphy, less happy, was captured and died on the gallows; so died Bagenal Harvey, of Barry Castle, and Anthony Perry, both Protestant gentlemen of fortune who had been forced into the rebellion, the one by Government suspicion, the other by imprisonment, cruelty, and torture. The revolution was crushed out with pitiless severity, until the deeds of the English soldiers and yeomanry became hateful in the eyes of the Viceroy himself, Lord Cornwallis. 'The conversation,' he writes in a letter to General Ross, 'of the principal persons of the country all tends to encourage the system of blood; and the conversation even at my table, where you will suppose I do all I can to prevent it, always turns on hanging, shooting, burning, etc., and if a priest has been put to death the greatest joy is expressed by the whole company. So much for Ireland and my wretched situation.'

Cornwallis acted mercifully. He proclaimed pardon to all insurgents guilty of rebellion only who should surrender their arms and take the oath of allegiance.

Of the State prisoners, the two brothers Sheares were hanged; McCann was hanged; Oliver Bond died in Newgate; O'Connor, Thomas Addis Emmet and McNevin were banished.

The insurrection was not quite over when a small French force, under General Humbert, landed in Killala Bay and entered Longford. But Humbert was surrounded by the English under Cornwallis and General Lake at Ballinamuck, and surrendered at discretion. The French were treated as prisoners of war, but the insurgent peasantry were slaughtered without quarter.

There was still one more scene in the drama of '98. A French squadron, under General Hardi, sailed for Ireland, but was attacked by an English squadron, and hopelessly defeated. Wolfe Tone, who was on board the principal vessel, the *Hoche*, was captured with the rest, and entertained with the French officers at Lord Cavan's house at Lough Swilly. Here a treacherous friend recognized him and addressed him by his name. Tone was too proud to affect concealment. He was at once sent in irons to Dublin, and tried by court-martial; he asked in vain for a soldier's death; he was condemned to be hanged, but he cut his throat in prison. The wound was not mortal, and he would have been hanged, had not Curran moved in the King's Bench for a writ of Habeas Corpus, on the ground that a court-martial had no jurisdiction while the Law Courts were still sitting in Dublin. The writ was granted, and Tone died a lingering death in prison.

Wolfe Tone was buried in Bodenstown, not far from the little village of Sallins, some eighteen miles from Dublin. Thomas Davis has devoted one of his finest lyrics to the green grave in Bodenstown churchyard, with the winter wind raving about it and the storm sweeping down on the plains of Kildare. The melancholy music of Davis's verse is well-suited to the desolate and deserted grass-grown graveyard and the little lonely church, ruined and roofless, and thickly grown with ivy, with the grave on the side away from the road. When Davis wrote his poem there was no stone upon the grave; now it is railed in with iron rails wrought at the top into the shape of shamrocks, and marked by a winter-worn headstone, and a stone slab with an inscription setting forth the name and deeds of the man who lies beneath, and ending 'God save Ireland.'

The leaders of constitutional agitation had taken no part in the rebellion of the United Irishmen. Neither Grattan nor Flood had belonged to the body, and neither of them had any sympathy with its efforts. They stood aside while the struggle was going on, and the most prominent place in the public mind was taken by a man not less gifted than either of them, John Curran. Like Grattan and like Flood, Curran began his career by trying to play on the double pipes of poetry and oratory, and like his great compeers he soon abandoned verse for prose. He rose from a very humble orgin, by the sheer force of his ability, to a commanding position at the Bar and an honourable position in Parliament, and his patriotism was never stained by the slightest political subservience. Before the rebellion of 1798 he had been conspicuous for his courage in advocating the causes of men unpopular with the Government and the English 'interest,' and after the rebellion broke out he rendered himself honourably eminent by the eloquence and the daring which he offered in turn to the cause of all the leading political prisoners. In his speech for Hamilton Rowan—a defence for which he was threatened like a new Cicero, but, unlike Cicero, remained undismayed—he made that defence of the principle of universal emancipation which has been so often, yet cannot be too often, quoted. 'I speak in the spirit of the British law, which makes liberty commensurate with, and inseparable from, the British soil, which proclaims even to the stranger and the sojourner, the moment he sets his foot on British earth, that the ground on which he treads is holy, and consecrated by the genius of universal emancipation. No matter in what language his doom may have been pronounced; no matter what complexion incompatible with freedom an African or an Indian sun may have burnt upon him; no matter in what disastrous battle his liberty may have been cloven down; no matter with what solemnities he may have been devoted upon the altar of slavery—the first moment he touches the sacred soil of Britain, the altar and the god sink together in the dust; his soul walks abroad in its own majesty, his body swells beyond the measure of his chains, that burst from around him, and he stands redeemed, regenerated, and disenthralled by the irresistible genius of universal emancipation.'

Appeals to the 'irresistible genius of universal emancipation' were not likely to have much effect just then. Martial and civil law vied with each other in severity towards the leaders of the United Irishmen. But these at least had striven for the cause of emancipation with arms in their hands. There was no such excuse to justify the measures now taken by the Government to ensure that the 'genius of universal emancipation,' however 'commensurate with, and inseparable from,' British soil, should have very little recognition on Irish earth.

Having destroyed the revolution, the Government now determined to destroy the Parliament. The liberty which Grattan had hoped might be perpetual, endured exactly eighteen years. Grattan had traced the career of Ireland from injuries to arms, and from arms to liberty. He was now to witness the reverse of the process, to watch the progress from liberty to arms, and from arms to injuries. The sword crushed out the rebellion, gold destroyed the Parliament. The ruin of the Irish Parliament is one of the most shameful stories of corruption and treachery of which history holds witness. It was necessary to obtain a Government majority in the Irish Parliament, and the majority was manufactured by the most unblushing bribery. The letters of Cornwallis confess the shame of a brave soldier at the unworthy means he had to employ in obeying the determination of the Government to steal from Ireland her newly-obtained liberties. Place and office were lavishly distributed. Peerages won the highest, and secret service money the lowest of those who were to be bought. The English Ministry had decided that Ireland was to be joined to England in an indissoluble union, and as Ireland was hostile to the scheme the union was effected by force and by fraud. The Bill of Union was introduced and passed by a well-paid majority of sixty in 1800. The eloquence of Grattan was raised to the last in immortal accents against the unholy pact. But the speech of angels would have been addressed in vain to the base and venal majority. It is something to remember that a hundred men could be found even in that degraded assembly whom the Ministry could not corrupt, who struggled to the last for the constitutional liberties of their country, and who did not abandon her in her agony.

It would not be well to leave this part of the story without a reference to the volumes which Mr. Froude has devoted to the 'English in Ireland in the Eighteenth Century.' There is perhaps no instance among the writings of history in which commanding talents have been put to a worse use. The deliberate and well-calculated intention of rousing up all the old animosities of race and religion, the carefully planned exaggeration of everything that tells against Ireland, and subordination or omission of all to be alleged in her favour, are evidence of a purpose to injure which happily defeats itself. The grotesque malignity with which Mr. Froude regards Ireland and everything Irish is so absurdly overdone, that, as Mr. Lecky says, 'his book has no more claim to impartiality than an election squib.' 'A writer of English history,' the words are Mr. Lecky's again, 'who took the "Newgate Calendar" as the most faithful expression of English ideas, and English murderers as the typical representatives of their nation, would not be regarded with unqualified respect.' Yet this is literally what Mr. Froude has done in his determined effort to envenom old wounds and rekindle the embers of old hatreds.

CHAPTER VIII.

EMMET. O'CONNELL.

Though the Union was accomplished with the opening of the century, the exchequers of the two countries were not consolidated for a score of years longer, during which Ireland suffered much, and England gained much by the new contract. England's superior command of capital rendered it impossible for Irish trade and enterprise to compete successfully with her while both were chained together under the same system, and as a natural consequence, Irish trade and enterprise dwindled, diminished, and practically disappeared. The Union, like too many compacts that have ever been made with the willing or unwilling Irish people, was immediately followed by a breach of faith. One of the most important factors in the securing of the Union was the pledge entered into by Pitt, and promulgated all over Ireland by print, that legislation on Catholic Emancipation and the Tithe Question would be introduced at once. It is not to be questioned that such a promise must have had great effect, if not in winning actual support to the scheme of Union, at least in preventing in many cases energetic opposition to it. To many the question of Catholic Emancipation was so immediately important, on many the grievous burden of the Tithe Question pressed so heavily, that they were almost ready to welcome any measure which offered to grant the one and relieve the other. But the pledge which Pitt had made Pitt could not fulfil. The bigoted and incapable monarch, who had opposed more reforms and brought more misfortune upon his own country than any other of all England's kings, stubbornly refused to give his consent to any measure for the relief of the Roman Catholics. Pitt immediately resigned, just eleven days after the Union had become law. The obstinate folly of the third George does not excuse the Minister, who had done his best to delude Ireland by arousing hopes which he was not certain of gratifying, and making pledges that he was unable to fulfil.

While the pledges to the Irish people were thus broken, the principles which had obtained before the Union remained unaltered. The system of corruption, which is perhaps inseparable from the Government of a Viceroy and a Castle clique, was in nowise diminished, and all the important offices of the Irish Executive were filled solely by Englishmen. But the deceived people could do nothing. The country was under martial law; and the experiences of '98 had left behind them a memorable lesson of what martial law meant. There was no means, as there would have been no use, in bringing forward their claims to consideration in any constitutional manner. But the strength of the national feeling of anger and despair may be estimated by the fact that, in spite of the horrors of the recent revolution, there were dangerous riots in several parts of Ireland, and that one actual rising took place, a last act of the rebellion of '98 surviving the Union. A young, brave, and gifted man, Robert Emmet, the youngest brother of Thomas Addis Emmet, planned the seizure of Dublin Castle. The rising failed. Emmet might have escaped, but he was in love with Sarah, Curran's daughter, and he was captured while awaiting an opportunity for an interview with her. Curran was bitterly opposed to the love affair; he refused to defend Emmet, and he has sometimes been accused in consequence of being indirectly the cause of Emmet's death. But we may safely assume that no counsel and no defence could have saved Emmet then. The trial was hurried through. Emmet was found guilty late at night. He was hanged the next morning, the 20th of September, 1803, in Thomas Street, on the spot where the gloomy church of St. Catherine looks down Bridgefoot Street, where his principal stores of arms had been found. Just before his death he wrote a letter to Richard, Curran's son, full of melancholy tenderness, regret for his lost love, and resignation for his untimely death:

'If there was anyone in the world in whose breast my death might be supposed not to stifle every spark of resentment, it might be you; I have deeply injured you —I have injured the happiness of a sister that you love, and who was formed to give happiness to everyone about her, instead of having her own mind a prey to affliction. Oh, Richard! I have no excuse to offer, but that I meant the reverse; I intended as much happiness for Sarah as the most ardent love could have given her. I never did tell you how much I idolized her; it was not with a wild or unfounded passion, but it was an attachment increasing every hour, from an admiration of the purity of her mind and respect for her talents. I did dwell in secret upon the prospect of our union. I did hope that success, while it afforded the opportunity of our union, might be the means of confirming an attachment which misfortune had called forth. I did not look to honours for myself—praise I would have asked from the lips of no man; but I would have wished to read in the glow of Sarah's countenance that her husband was respected. My love! Sarah! it was not thus that I thought to have requited your affection. I had hoped to be a prop, round which your affections might have clung, and which would never have been shaken; but a rude blast has snapped it, and they have fallen over a grave.'

The Government acted against all the persons concerned in Emmet's rising with a rigour such as only panic could inspire. The fear of a French invasion was incessantly before the eyes of the English Government, and for several years the Habeas Corpus Act was suspended, and an Insurrection Act in full force. But they took no steps whatever to allay the discontent which alone could inspire and animate such insurrections. Pitt returned to office in 1804 on the distinct understanding that he would no longer weary the King with suggestions of relief for the Irish Catholics, and the Minister kept his word. The helplessness of the Irish Catholics and the obvious indifference of the Government to their condition, now fostered the formation of a powerful anti-Catholic association, the Orange Society, a body organized to support the Crown so long as it supported Protestant ascendancy in Ireland, and which at one time in later years in England seems to have gone near to shifting the succession of the Crown altogether.

For years the government of Ireland drifted along on its old course of corruption and indifference. Pitt died, and Fox took his place. But the genius of the great statesman, 'on whose burning tongue truth, peace, and freedom hung,' was quenched within the year, and with it the only spirit of statesmanship which understood and sympathized with the struggles of the Irish people. These struggles were carried on in straggling continuity, in the form of vain petitions for redress from the Catholics of the better class, and of frequent disturbances of a more or less desperate kind on the part of the peasantry. In 1807 the tithe and land difficulties created two bodies, known as Shanavests and Caravats, who seem to have agitated for a time very fiercely before they disappeared under the pressure of the law. But once again, after a decade of despair, a new leader of the Irish people, a new champion of the Catholic demands for freedom and the rights of citizenship, came upon the scene.

Daniel O'Connell was the first Irish leader for many years who was himself a Roman Catholic. In 1807 he had made his first political appearance as a member of the committee appointed to present the petitions setting forth the Catholic claims to Parliament. In 1810 his name came more prominently before the public as a speaker at a meeting called by the Protestant Corporation of Dublin to petition for the repeal of the Union. He at once began to take a prominent part in the Emancipation Movement, which grew in strength and determination year by year. Catholic meetings were held, and were dispersed by the Government time after time, but still the agitation went on. Its chief supporters in Parliament were Henry Grattan, now an old man, and Sir Henry Parnell. In 1820 Grattan died, but the cause to which he devoted his life was rapidly striding towards success. O'Connell and Richard

Lalor Sheil, an advocate as enthusiastic, an orator only less powerful than O'Connell himself, were bringing the cause nearer and nearer to its goal. Three Bills, embracing Emancipation, disfranchisement of the forty shilling householder freeholders, and the payment of the Roman Catholic Clergy, were introduced and advanced in the House of Commons; but the House of Lords, urged by the Duke of York's 'So help me God' speech against the Bills, was resolutely opposed to them. The triumph was only postponed. The agitators discovered that the Act which prohibited Roman Catholics from sitting in Parliament said nothing against their being elected, and O'Connell prepared to carry the war into Westminster. In 1828 he was returned to the House of Commons for Clare county. He refused to take the oath, which was expressly framed to exclude Catholics from the House. His refusal caused great agitation in both countries, and resulted in the passing of the Bill for Catholic Emancipation in 1829, after which O'Connell took his seat. To O'Connell what may be considered as the Parliamentary phase of the Irish Movement is due. He first brought the forces of constitutional agitation in England to bear upon the Irish Question, and showed what great results might be obtained thereby.

The Act for the relief of his Majesty's Roman Catholic subjects abolished all oaths and declarations against transubstantiation, the invocation of saints, and the sacrifice of the mass; it allowed all Roman Catholics, except priests, to sit and vote in the House of Commons, and made no such exception for the House of Lords. A special form of oath was devised for Roman Catholic members of Parliament, the chief provision of which called upon them to maintain the Protestant succession of the House of Hanover, and to make no effort to weaken the Protestant religion.

Though O'Connell had been the means of calling the Act into existence, he was not yet able to take his seat. The Act had been passed since his election for Clare; its action was not retrospective. When he presented himself to be sworn, the old oath, which it was impossible for him to take, was presented to him. He refused it, and was called upon to withdraw. After some debate he was heard at the bar of the House. There was a division, and his right to take the new oath was negatived by 190 to 116. A new writ was issued for Clare. O'Connell was, of course, re-elected without opposition, and took his seat and the new oath on the 4th of February, 1830. But between O'Connell's first and second election a change had been made in the composition of the electors. By an Act of Henry VIII., which had been confirmed in 1795, freeholders to the value of forty shillings over and above all charges were entitled to vote, a system which naturally created an immense number of small landowners, who were expected to vote in obedience to the landlords who created them. O'Connell's election showed that the landlords could not always command the forty shilling voters. It was clear that they might be won over to any popular movement, and it was decided to abolish them, which was accordingly done by an Act passed on the same day with the Catholic Emancipation Act. The new Act raised the county franchise to ten pounds, and freeholders of ten pounds, but under twenty pounds, were subjected to a complicated system of registration, well calculated to bewilder the unhappy tenant and render his chance of voting more difficult. But all these precautions did not prevent the triumphant return of O'Connell the second time he appealed to the electors of Clare, nor did it ever prove of much service in repressing the tenants from voting for the leaders of popular movements.

The disenfranchisement produced intense discontent throughout the country, and disorder followed close on discontent. O'Connell now began to remind Ireland of his promise that Catholic Emancipation was a means towards an end, and that end the repeal of the Union. He started a society called the 'Friend of Ireland,' which the Government at once put down. He started another, 'The Anti-Union Association.' It was put down too, and O'Connell was arrested for sedition, tried, and found guilty. Judgment was deferred and never pronounced, and O'Connell was released to carry on his agitation more vigorously than ever. With Ireland torn by disorders against which even the Insurrection Acts in force found it hard to cope, with the country aflame with anger at the extinction of the forty shilling vote, the Government judged it wise and prudent to bring in a Bill for Ireland in January, 1832, effecting still further disfranchisement. The new Bill abolished the forty shilling vote in boroughs as well as in counties, and the lowest rate for boroughs and counties was ten pounds.

But for the next few years all recollection of emancipation on the one hand, and disenfranchisement on the other, was to be swallowed up in a struggle which has passed into history as the Irish Tithe War. The English Church was established in Ireland against the will of the enormous majority of the Irish people, and they were compelled to pay tithes to maintain the obnoxious establishment. Sidney Smith declared that there was no abuse like this in Timbuctoo, and he estimated that probably a million of lives had been sacrificed in Ireland to the collection of tithes. They had to be wrung from the reluctant people at the point of the bayonet, and often enough by musket volleys. There were naturally incessant riots. The clergymen of the Established Church had to call in the services of an army, and appeal to the strategies and menaces of miniature war to obtain their tithes from the harassed followers of another faith. Such a state of things could not last long. In the end a general strike against the payment of tithes was organized, and then not all the king's horses nor all the king's men could have enforced their payment. In 1833 the arrears of tithes exceeded a mil lion and a quarter of money. There was in Ireland an army almost as great as that which held India. In 1833 it had cost more than a million to maintain this army, with £300,000 more for the police force, and the Government had spent £26,000 to collect £12,000 of tithes. For many years successive English ministers and statesmen made efforts to deal with the Tithes Question; but it was not until 1838, a year after Queen Victoria came to the throne, that a Bill was passed by Lord John Russell, which converted tithes into a rent charge, recoverable from the landlord instead of from the tenant. The tenant had practically still to pay the tithes in increased rent to his landlord, but it was no longer levied from him directly as tithes, and by the ministers of the Established Church; that was the only difference. It only exasperated the existing discontent. The agitation turned against rent, now that the rent meant tithes as well. Secret societies increased. A landlord, Lord Norbury, was assassinated, and the assassins were never discovered, though the country was under severe Coercion Acts.

In the year 1845 there was fierce discussion in England over the Maynooth grant. Some time before the Union a Government grant had been made to the Roman Catholic college at Maynooth, where young men who wished to become priests were educated. But the old grant was insufficient, and Sir Robert Peel increased it in the teeth of the most violent opposition, not merely from his political opponents, but from many who were on other matters his political partizans. Mr. Gladstone resigned his place in the Ministry rather than countenance the increased Maynooth grant. For years and years after, annual motions were made in the House of Commons for the withdrawal of the grant, and wearily debated until the abolition of the State Church in Ireland abolished the grant too and ended the matter. Peel also established the Queen's Colleges of Cork, Belfast, and Galway, for purely secular teaching, which came to be known in consequence as the Godless Colleges. These colleges pleased neither Catholics nor Protestants. The Catholics argued that there were universities which gave Protestants religious as well as secular education, and that the Catholics should be allowed something of the same kind. Still the new scheme at least allowed Catholics an opportunity of obtaining a university education and winning university degrees. Up to that time no Irishman of the religion of his race could win any of the honours that the universities of Ireland offered which were worth winning. He might indeed enter their gates and sit at the feet of their teachers, but so long as he was a Catholic he could practically reap no rewards for his scholarship.

O'Connell's success in winning Catholic emancipation inspired him with the desire to bring about the repeal of the Union, and it did not seem to him and his followers that the difficulties in the way were any greater than those which had showed so terrible when Catholic Emancipation was first demanded, and which had been triumphantly overcome.

There was a great deal against the agitation. To begin with, the country was very poor. 'Every class of the community,' says Sir Charles Gavan Duffy, 'were poorer than the corresponding class in any country in Europe.' The merchants, who had played a prominent part in political life since the Union, were now wearied and despairing of all agitation, and held aloof; the Protestant gentry were, for the most part, devoted to the Union; many of the Catholic gentry disliked O'Connell himself and his rough wild ways; many of O'Connell's old associates in the Catholic Emancipation movement had withdrawn from him to join the Whigs. In England the most active dislike of O'Connell prevailed. The Pericles or the Socrates of Aristophanes, the royalists drawn by Camille Desmoulins, were not grotesquer caricatures than the representation of O'Connell by English opinion and the English press.

But on the other hand there was much for O'Connell. It might be said of him as of Wordsworth's Toussaint l'Ouverture, that 'his friends were exultations, agonies, and love, and man's unconquerable mind.' The people were with him, the people to whose sufferings he appealed, the people for whom he had secured the Catholic Emancipation, and who regarded him as almost invincible. He was a great orator, endowed with a wonderful voice, which he could send in all its strength and sweetness to the furthest limits of the vastest crowd that ever came together to hear him speak. Lord Lytton declared that he first learned

'What spells of infinite choice
To rouse or lull has the sweet human voice,'

when he heard O'Connell speak, and that in watching him governing with his genius and his eloquence one of his great meetings, he learned

> 'To seize the sudden clue,
> To the grand troublous life antique, to view
> Under the rock stand of Demosthenes
> Unstable Athens heave her stormy seas.'

It was not unnatural that O'Connell should have been carried away by his triumph and the homage his country gave him everywhere into the belief that the repeal of the Union was to be as easily accomplished by the strong man and the determined nation as the emancipation of the Catholics.

During the years of disturbance and repression, O'Connell had let the demand for repeal lie comparatively quiet, but it was gradually gaining strength and popularity throughout the country. It was supported at first by the *Nation* newspaper. In 1843 the Repeal Association was founded; O'Connell contrived to enlist in its ranks Father Mathew, and the large number of followers Father Mathew was daily winning over to the cause of total abstinence.

'The year 1843,' said O'Connell, 'is and shall be the great repeal year.' The prediction was vain; forty years have gone by, and still the Union holds; O'Connell had Ireland at his back; he convened gigantic meetings where every word of his wonderful voice was treasured as the utterance of a prophet; but when the agitation had reached a height which seemed dangerous to the Government, and made them decide to put it down, his power was over. He would sanction no sort of physical force, no opposition other than constitutional opposition to the Government. The Government proclaimed his meetings and put him into prison; he was soon set free, but his reign was over. Fierce spirits had risen in his place, men who scornfully repudiated the abnegation of physical force. Broken in health, O'Connell turned to Rome, and died on the way, at Genoa, on May 15th, 1847. Many recent political writers have been at the pains to glorify O'Connell at the expense of later leaders. It is instructive to remember that in O'Connell's life-time, and for long after, he was the object of political hatred and abuse, no less unsparing than any that has assailed his successors in Irish popularity.

The condition of Ireland at the time of O'Connell's death was truly desperate. From 1845 to 1847 a terrible famine had been literally laying the country waste. The chief, indeed practically the only food of the Irish peasantry then, as now, was the potato, and a failure of the potato crop meant starvation. 'But what,' says Carlyle in his French Revolution, 'if history somewhere on this planet were to hear of a nation, the third soul of whom had not for thirty weeks each year as many third rate potatoes as would sustain him? History, in that case, feels bound to consider that starvation is starvation; that starvation from age to age presupposes much; History ventures to assert that the French Sansculotte of '93, who, roused from long death-sleep could rush at once to the frontiers, and die fighting for an immortal hope and faith of deliverance for him and his, was but the second miserablest of men! The Irish Sans-potato, had he not senses then, nay, a soul? In his frozen darkness it was bitter for him to die famishing, bitter to see his children famish.'

In 1845, 1846, and in 1847, the potato crop had failed, and for the time the country seemed almost given over to hunger and to death. Thousands died miserably from starvation; thousands fled across the seas, seeking refuge in America, to hand down to their children and their children's children, born in the American Republic, a bitter recollection of the misery they had endured, and the wrongs that had been inflicted upon them. When the famine was at an end it was found that Ireland had lost two millions of population. Before the famine she had eight millions, now she had six. All through the famine the Government had done nothing; private charity in England, in America, even in Turkey, had done something, and done it nobly, to stay the desolation and the dissolution that the famine was causing. But the Government, if it could not appease the famine, showed itself active in devising Coercion Bills to put down any spirit of violence which misery and starvation might haply have engendered in the Irish people.

Such was the condition of the country when O'Connell and the Repeal Movement died together, and when the Young Ireland Movement, with its dream of armed rebellion, came into existence.

CHAPTER IX.

YOUNG IRELAND—FENIANISM.

THE *Nation* newspaper was first published on the 13th October, 1842; it was founded by Gavan Duffy, John Blake Dillon, and Thomas Davis. Gavan Duffy was the editor, but he says himself, in his history of the movement, that Davis was their true leader. They were all young men; Davis was twenty-eight, Dillon twenty-seven, and Duffy twenty-six. Davis, says Sir Charles Gavan Duffy, 'was a man of middle stature, strongly but not coarsely built .... a broad brow and strong jaw stamped his face with a character of power; but except when it was lighted by thought or feeling, it was plain and even rugged.' In his boyhood, he was 'shy, retiring, unready, and self-absorbed,' was even described as 'a dull child' by unappreciative kinsfolk. At Trinity College he was a wide and steady reader, who was chiefly noted by his fellow students for his indifference to rhetorical display. He was auditor of the Dublin Historical Society, had made some name for himself by his contributions to a magazine called the *Citizen*, and was a member of the Repeal Association. When Duffy made John Dillon's acquaintance, Dillon was 'tall, and strikingly handsome, with eyes like a thoughtful woman's, and the clear olive complexion and stately bearing of a Spanish nobleman.' He had been designed for the priesthood, but had decided to adopt the bar. Like Davis, he loved intellectual pursuits, and was a man of wide and varied learning. 'Under a stately and somewhat reserved demeanour lay latent the simplicity and joyfulness of a boy; no one was readier to laugh with frank cordiality, or to give and take the pleasant banter which lends a relish to the friendship of young men.' Long years after, Thackeray said of him to Gavan Duffy, that the modesty and wholesome sweetness of John Dillon gave him a foremost place among the half dozen men in the United States whom he loved to remember.

The success of the *Nation* was extraordinary. Its political teachings, its inspiring and vigorous songs and ballads, the new lessons of courage and hope which it taught, the wide knowledge of history possessed by its writers,—all combined to make it welcome to thousands. The tradesmen in town and the country peasants read it, and were animated by the story of their old historic island into the belief that she had a future, and that the future was close at hand, and that they were to help to make it. It was denounced by the Tory press as the organ of a hidden 'French party.' From France itself came words of praise worth having from two Irish officers in the French service. One was Arthur O'Connor, the Arthur O'Connor of '98; the other was Miles Byrne, who had fought at Wexford. O'Connell became alarmed at the growing popularity of the *Nation*. At first it had strongly supported him: he had even written a Repeal Catechism in its pages; but its young men had the courage to think for themselves, and to criticize even the deeds and words of the Liberator. More and more young men clustered around the writers of the *Nation*; brilliant young essayists, politicians, poets. Gifted women wrote for the *Nation*, too—Lady Wilde, 'Speranza,' chief among them. The songs published in a volume called 'The Spirit of the Nation,' became immediately very popular. As the agitation grew, Peel's Government became more threatening. O'Connell, in most of his defiant declarations, evidently thought that Peel did not dare to put down the organization for Repeal, or he would never have challenged him as he did; for O'Connell never really meant to resort to force at any time. But the few young men who wrote for the *Nation*, and the many young men who read the *Nation*, were really prepared to fight if need be for their liberties. Nor did they want foreign sympathy to encourage them. In the United States vast meetings, organized and directed by men like Seward and Horace Greeley, threatened England with 'the assured loss of

Canada by American arms,' if she suppressed the Repeal agitation by force; and later Horace Greeley was one of a Directory in New York for sending officers and arms to Ireland. In France, the Republican Party were loud in their expressions of sympathy for the Irish, and Ledru Rollin had declared that France was ready to lend her strength to the support of an oppressed nation. No wonder the leaders of the National Party were encouraged in the belief that their cause was pleasing to the fates.

A new man now began to come forward as a prominent figure in Irish politics, Mr. William Smith O'Brien, Member of Parliament for Limerick county. He was a country gentleman of stately descent, a direct descendant of Brian Boroimhe, a brother of Lord Inchiquin. He was a high-minded and honourable gentleman, with his country's cause deeply at heart. Davis described him as the 'most extravagant admirer of the *Nation* I have ever met.' Another prominent man was John Mitchel, the son of an Ulster Unitarian minister. When O'Connell's vast agitation fell to pieces after the suppression of the meeting of Clontarf, and the subsequent imprisonment of O'Connell showed that the Liberator did not mean ever to appeal to the physical force he had talked about, these two men became the leaders of different sections of the Young Ireland Party, as the men of the *Nation* were now called. Thomas Davis, the sweet chief singer of the movement, died suddenly before the movement which he had done so much for had taken direct revolutionary shape. Mitchel came on the *Nation* in his place, and advocated Revolution and Republicanism. He followed the traditions of Emmet and the men of '98; he was in favour of independence. His doctrines attracted the more ardent of the Young Irelanders, and what was known as a war party was formed. There were now three sections of Irish agitation. There were the Repealers, who were opposed to all physical force; there were the moderate Young Irelanders, only recognising physical force when all else had failed in the last instance; and there were now this new party who saw in revolution the only remedy for

Ireland. Smith O'Brien was bitterly opposed to Mitchel's doctrines. Mitchel withdrew from the *Nation* and started a paper of his own, the *United Irishman*, in which he advocated them more fiercely than ever. But though most of the Young Irelanders were not so extreme as Mitchel, the great majority of them talked, wrote, and thought revolution. In passionate poems and eloquent speeches they expressed their hatred of tyranny and their stern resolve to free their country by brave deeds rather than by arguments. They had now a brilliant orator among them, Thomas Francis Meagher, 'a young man,' says Mr. Lecky, 'whose eloquence was beyond comparison superior to that of any other rising speaker in the country, and who, had he been placed in circumstances favourable to the development of his talent, might perhaps, at length, have taken his place among the great orators of Ireland.' Meagher had early endeared himself to the impetuous and gifted young men with whom he was allied, by a brilliant speech against O'Connell's doctrine of passive resistance. 'I am not one of those tame moralists,' the young man exclaimed, 'who say that liberty is not worth one drop of blood. . . . Against this miserable maxim the noble virtue that has saved and sanctified humanity appears in judgment. From the blue waters of the Bay of Salamis; from the valley over which the sun stood still and lit the Israelites to victory; from the cathedral in which the sword of Poland has been sheathed in the shroud of Kosciusko; from the Convent of St. Isidore, where the fiery hand that rent the ensign of St. George upon the plains of Ulster has mouldered into dust; from the sands of the desert, where the wild genius of the Algerine so long has scared the eagle of the Pyrenees; from the ducal palace in this kingdom, where the memory of the gallant and seditious Geraldine enhances more than royal favour the splendour of his race; from the solitary grave within this mute city which a dying bequest has left without an epitaph—oh! from every spot where heroism has had a sacrifice or a triumph, a voice breaks in upon the cringing crowd that cherishes this maxim, crying, "Away with it—away with it."' The year 1848, the year of unfulfilled revolutions, when crowns were falling and kings flying about in all directions, might well have seemed a year of happy omen for a new Irish rebellion. But the Young Irelanders were not ready for rebellion when their plans were made known to Government, and the Government struck at them before they could do anything. Mitchel was arrested, tried, and transported to Bermuda. That was the turning-point of the Revolution. The Mitchelites wished to rise in rescue. They urged, and rightly urged, that if revolution was meant at all, then was the time. But the less extreme men held back. An autumnal rising had been decided upon, and they were unwilling to anticipate the struggle. They carried their point. Mitchel was sentenced to fourteen years' transportation. When the verdict was delivered he declared that, like the Roman Scævola, he could promise hundreds who would follow his example, and as he spoke he pointed to John Martin, Meagher, and others of the associates who were thronging the galleries of the court. A wild cry came up from all his friends, 'Promise for me, Mitchel—promise for me!' With that cry ringing in his ears he was hurried from the court, heavily ironed and encircled by a little army of dragoons, to the war-sloop *Shearwater*, that had been waiting for the verdict and the man. As the war-sloop steamed out of Dublin harbour the hopes of the Young Irelanders went with her, vain and evanescent, from that hour forth, as the smoke that floated in the steamer's wake. Mitchel had himself discountenanced, to his undying honour, any attempt at rescue. There is a pathetic little story which records his looking out of the prison-van that drove him from the court, and seeing a great crowd and asking where they were going, and being told that they were going to a flower-show. There were plenty of men in the movement who would have gladly risked everything to try and rescue Mitchel. But nothing could have been done without unanimity, and the too great caution of the leaders prevented the effort at the only moment when it could have had the faintest hope of success. From that hour the movement was doomed.

Men who had gone into the revolution heart and soul might then have said of Smith O'Brien, as Menas in 'Antony and Cleopatra' says to Pompey, 'For this I'll never follow thy pall'd fortunes more. Who seeks and will not take when once 'tis offered, shall never find it more.' The supreme moment of danger thus passed over, the Government lost no time in crushing out all that was left of the insurrection. Smith O'Brien, Meagher and Dillon went down into the country, and tried to raise an armed rebellion. There was a small scuffle with the police in a cabbage-garden at Ballingarry, in Tipperary; the rebels were dispersed, and the rebellion was over. Smith O'Brien, Meagher and others were arrested and condemned to death. Meagher's speech from the dock was worthy of his rhetorical genius. 'I am not here to crave with faltering lip the life I have consecrated to the independence of my country. . . . . I offer to my country, as some proof of the sincerity with which I have thought and spoken and struggled for her, the life of a young heart. . . . . The history of Ireland explains my crime and justifies it. . . . . Even here, where the shadows of death surround me, and from which I see my early grave opening for me in no consecrated soil, the hope which beckoned me forth on that perilous sea whereon I have been wrecked, animates, consoles, enraptures me. No, I don't despair of my poor old country, her peace, her liberty, her glory!'

The death sentence was commuted to transportation for life, and some years after Mitchel and Meagher succeeded in escaping from Australia, and later on Smith O'Brien was pardoned, and died in Wales in 1854. Mitchel was elected to the House of Commons years after, and was not allowed to sit, and died whilst the question was still pending. Meagher fought bravely for the cause of the North in the American Civil War, and died ingloriously, drowned in the muddy waters of the Missouri. Gavan Duffy was tried three times, but could not be convicted. He afterwards sat for some time in Parliament, and then went into voluntary exile, to find fame and fortune in Victoria. For sixteen years the country was politically quiet. A vain attempt was made in 1849, after all the Young Ireland leaders had fled or been sent into exile, to revive the agitation and re-create the insurrection. A few abortive local risings there were, and nothing more. Starvation and misery forced the people into steady and incessant emigration. Eviction was in full swing, and between eviction and emigration it is estimated that almost a million of people left Ireland between 1847 and 1857. 'In a few years more,' said the *Times* exultingly, 'a Celtic Irishman will be as rare in Connemara as is the Red Indian on the shores of Manhattan.' That the *Times* was not a true prophet was no fault of the majority of the Irish landlords. Evictions took place by the hundred, by the thousand, by the ten thousand. Winter or summer, day or night, fair or foul weather, the tenants were ejected. Sick or well, bedridden or dying, the tenants, men, women or children, were turned out for the rents they had not paid, for the rents which in those evil days of famine and failure they could not pay. They might go to America if they could; they might die on the roadstead if so it pleased them. They were out of the hut, and the hut was unroofed that they might not seek its shelter again, and that was all the landlord cared about. The expiring evicted tenant might, said Mitchel, raise his dying eyes to heaven and bless his God that he perished under the finest constitution in the world. It is hardly a matter of surprise, however much of regret and reprobation, that the lives of the evicting landlords should often be in peril, and often be taken. The English farmer, the English cottier, have happily no idea of the horror of evictions in Ireland as they prevailed in the years that followed the famine of 1847, as they had always prevailed, as they prevail still.

Many of the landlords themselves were in no enviable condition. Mortgages and settlements of all kinds, the results of their own or their ancestors' profuseness, hung on their estates and made many a stately-showing rent-roll the merest simulacrum of territorial wealth. Even rack rents could not enable many of the landlords to keep their heads above water. At length the English Government made an effort to relieve their condition by passing the Encumbered Estates Act, by means of which a landlord or his creditors might petition to have an estate sold in the Court established for that purpose under the Act. In 1858, by a supplementary Irish Landed Estates Act, the powers of the Court were increased to allow the sale of properties that were not encumbered.

The tenant wanted legislation as well as the landlord, and in August, 1850, those who sympathized with the tenant's cause began to agitate for legislation. A conference was called by Dr. (afterwards Sir) John Gray, the Protestant owner of the *Freeman's Journal*, by the Presbyterian barrister Mr. Greer, who later represented Derry in Parliament, and by Frederick Lucas, the Catholic owner of the *Tablet*. A conference of men of all classes and creeds was held in Dublin—a conference Mr. Bright then called it in the House of Commons 'of earnest men from all parts of Ireland,' and a tenant league was started. Everything was against the league. The indifference of England, the prostration of the country after the famine and the rebellion, the apathy, even the hostility of the Irish Liberal Members, were all combined against it. Then came the reorganization of the Catholic Church in England, and Lord John Russell's 'Durham Letter,' which for the time made any political alliance between Catholic and Protestant impossible. But when, in 1852, the Whig Ministry went out and Lord Derby, coming in with the Tories, dissolved Parliament, the chance of the tenant leaguers came. Some fifty tenant-right Members were elected. There was a Tenant Right Party in the House of Commons, 'the Irish Brigade' it came to be called, but it did little good to the cause of tenant right. Its leader was the once famous John Sadleir; his lieutenants were his brother James, Mr. William Keogh, and Mr. Edmond O'Flaherty; these men were all adventurers and most of them swindlers. For a time they deceived the Irish people by their professions and protestations. The Sadleirs owned the Tipperary Bank, one of the most popular banks in Ireland; they had plenty of money, and spent it lavishly; they started a paper, the *Telegraph*, to keep them before the public; they were good speakers, and they led good speakers; they were demonstratively Catholic, and for a time a good many people believed in them, though they were of course distrusted by most intelligent Irishmen.

In November Lord Derby went out of office and Whig Lord Aberdeen came in, and the leaders of the noisy, blatant brass band took office under him. John Sadleir became a Lord of the Treasury; Keogh was made Irish Solicitor-General; O'Flaherty Commissioner of Income Tax. There was fierce indignation, but they kept their places and their course for a time. Then they broke up. John Sadleir had embezzled, swindled, forged; he ruined half Ireland with his fraudulent bank; he made use of his position under Government to embezzle public money; he committed suicide. His brother was expelled from the House of Commons; he fled the country and was heard of no more. O'Flaherty hurried to Denmark, where there was no extradition treaty, and then to New York. Keogh, the fourth of this famous quadrilateral, their ally, their intimate, their faithful friend, contrived to keep himself clear of the crash. He was immediately made a judge, and was conspicuous for the rest of his life for his unfailing and unaltering hostility to any and every Irish national party.

Once again there was a period of political apathy, as far as constitutional agitation was concerned. But the '48 rebellion had left rebellious seed behind it. Even as the United Irishmen had generated Repeal, and Repeal Young Ireland, so Young Ireland generated the Phœnix Conspiracy, and the Phœnix Conspiracy soon grew into the Fenian Brotherhood, a vast organization with members in all parts of the world, with money at its disposal, and more money, with soldiers trained by the American Civil War. Irish Americans steadily promulgated the cause in Ireland, and prepared for the rising. The Fenians in America invaded Canada on the 31st May, 1866, occupied Fort Erie, defeated the

Canadian volunteers, and captured some flags. But the United States interfered to enforce the neutrality of their frontier, arrested most of the leaders, and extinguished the invasion. The Fenians in England planned the capture of Chester Castle; the scheme was to seize the arms in the castle, to hasten on to Holyhead, to take possession of such steamers as might be there, and invade Ireland before the authorities in Ireland could be prepared for the blow; but the plan was betrayed and failed. Then in March, 1867, an attempt at a general rising was made in Ireland, and failed completely; the very elements fought against it. Snow, rare in Ireland, fell incessantly, and practically buried the rising in its white shroud. Large numbers of prisoners were taken in England and Ireland and sentenced to penal servitude. In Manchester two Fenian prisoners were released from the prison van by some armed Fenians, and in the scuffle a policeman was killed. For this, three of the rescuers, Allen, Larkin, and O'Brien, were hanged. Mr. John Stuart Mill and Mr. Bright strove hard to save their lives, with all the eloquence and all the influence they could bring to bear. Mr. Swinburne addressed a noble and equally unsuccessful poetic 'Appeal' to England to 'put forth her strength, and release,' for which his name should be held in eternal honour by the people of Ireland.

A little later a wicked and foolish attempt was made to blow up the Clerkenwell Prison in order to set free some imprisoned Fenians. It failed to do this, but it killed some innocent persons, and its perpetrator was hanged.

But the succession of these events had convinced a statesman, who came into power shortly after, that the condition of Ireland urgently called for remedial legislation. The Parliament which met at the close of 1868, under Mr. Gladstone's leadership in the House of Commons, was known to be prepared to deal with some of the most pressing of Irish questions; of these the foremost was the Irish State Church. It is not necessary to enter at any length into the history of the manner in which Mr. Gladstone accomplished the disestablishment and the disendowment of the State Church in Ireland. It is sufficient here to record the fact that it was disestablished and disendowed. For centuries it had been one of the bitterest emblems of oppression in Ireland. In a country of which the vast majority were Catholic, it had been, in the words of Lord Sherbrooke, then Mr. Lowe, 'kept alive with the greatest difficulty and at the greatest expense.' It was an exotic with the curse of barrenness upon it, and Mr. Lowe called upon the Government to 'cut it down; why cumbereth it the ground?' The Government replied to the appeal, and the State Church in Ireland ceased to exist. This done, Mr. Gladstone turned his attention to the Irish Land Question, a very pressing question indeed.

CHAPTER X.

THE LAND QUESTION.

In all the melancholy chronicles of Irish misery and disaffection, and of unsuccessful English measures to remedy the misery and to coerce the disaffection, the land plays an important part.

After the incessant confiscations and settlements of Irish soil, the vast majority of the Irish people were reduced to the condition of mere tenants-at-will of landlords who were either foreigners in fact or in sympathy. The majority of the landlords were actuated only by the desire to get as high a price as they could for their land, and the need of land was so imperative to the Irish peasant, who had nothing but the land to live upon; that he was ready to take any terms, no matter how terrible. Of course, he could not often pay the terms exacted. The rack-rent begot the eviction, and the eviction begot the secret societies, the Ribbon lodges, which the Irish peasant began to look upon as his sole protection against landlord tyranny. What exactly were these Ribbon lodges, which are so often named in all accounts of the Irish Land Question? For more than half a century the Ribbon Society has existed in Ireland, and even yet it is impossible to say for certain how it began, how it is organized, and what are its exact purposes. Its aim seems to have been chiefly to defend the landserf from the landlord, but it often had a strong political purpose as well. Mr. A. M. Sullivan, in his 'New Ireland,' states that he long ago satisfied himself that the Ribbonism of one period was not the Ribbonism of another, and that the version of its aims and character prevalent amongst its members in one part of Ireland often differed widely from those professed in some other part of the country. 'In Ulster it professed to be a defensive or retaliatory league against Orangeism; in Munster it was at first a combination against tithe-proctors; in Connaught it was an organization against rack-renting and evictions; in Leinster it was often mere trade-unionism, dictating by its mandates and enforcing by its vengeance the employment or dismissal of workmen, stewards, and even domestics.' All sorts of evidence and information of the most confused kind has been from time to time given with respect to Ribbonism, much of it the merest fiction. All that is certain is that it and many other formidable defensive organizations existed among the peasantry of different parts of Ireland.

Perhaps Ireland was the only country in the world in which a man had nothing to gain by improving the land he lived upon. If he improved it, he was certain in nine cases out of ten to have his rent raised upon him as a reward for his labour. He was absolutely at the mercy, or rather the want of mercy, of his landlord, whom he perhaps had never seen, for many of the landlords were absentees, living out of Ireland on the money they took from the country. The Irish peasant's misery did not pass altogether unnoticed. Ever since the Union, Select Committees had again and again reported the distress in the fullest manner. Too often the report was left to lie in bulky oblivion upon the dusty shelves of State libraries, or was answered by a coercive measure. No attempt was made for many years to feed the famished peasant or to relieve the evicted tenant. Legislation only sought to make sure that while their complaints were unheeded their hands should be stayed from successful revenge. The greatest concession that Government made for many generations to the misery of the Irish tenant was to pass an Act prohibiting evictions on Christmas Day and Good Friday, and enacting that the roof of a tenant's house should not be pulled off until the inmates had left.

A Select Committee was appointed in 1819, under the presidency of Sir John Newton, which reported on the great misery of the labouring poor, and unavailingly urged agricultural reform, especially advising the reclamation of waste lands. Another Committee reported in 1823 that the condition of the people was miserable, and also unsuccessfully urged the importance of some form of agricultural relief. Two years later, in 1825, a fresh Select Committee gave fresh evidence as to the misery of the country, and made fresh suggestions that something should be done for the Irish tenant, and, as before, nothing was done. The Act of 1793, giving every forty shilling freeholder a vote, had indirectly injured the people, as the landlords leased small patches of land to increase their political power. The Emancipation Act of 1829, abolishing the vote of the forty shilling freeholder, removed with it the landlord's interest in small holdings, and so again caused misery to the people by its introduction of the system of clearances.. In 1829 the condition of the tenant farmers and labouring classes of Ireland was brought forcibly under the notice of the Government by Mr. Brownlow, who went so far as to ask leave to bring in a Bill to facilitate the reclamation of waste lands. The Bill passed the Commons, and was read a second time in the Lords. It was then referred to a Select Committee, and heard of no more. But, on the other hand, an Arms Bill, which an English peer was found to denounce as vexatious and aggressive, was successfully carried. In 1830 Mr. Henry Grattan, son of Ireland's great orator, and Mr. Spring Rice, afterwards Lord Monteagle, urged the sufferings of Ireland upon the Government, and strongly advocated the reclamation of waste lands. But nothing whatever was done beyond the appointment of a Select Committee. This Select Committee of 1830 had the same story to tell that all its unfortunate predecessors told. It appealed in vain.

The valuation of Ireland was undertaken in 1830 on the recommendation of a Select Committee of the House of Commons in 1824. To ensure uniform valuation, an Act was passed in 1836 requiring all valuations of land to be based on a fixed scale of agricultural produce contained in the Act. The valuators were instructed to act in the same manner as if employed by a principal landlord dealing with a solvent tenant. The average valuation proved to be about twenty-five per cent under the gross rental of the country. In 1844 a Select Committee of the House of Commons was appointed to reconsider the question, and an Act passed in 1846 changed the principle of valuation from a relative valuation of town lands based on a fixed scale of agricultural produce to a tenement valuation for poor law rating to be made 'upon an estimate of the net annual value .... of the rent, for which, one year with another, the same might in its actual state be reasonably expected to let from year to year.' The two valuations gave substantially the same results. In 1852 another Valuation Act was passed, returniug to the former principle of valuation by a fixed scale of agricultural produce; but Sir Richard Griffiths' evidence in 1869 shows the valuation employed was a 'live-and-let-live valuation, according to the state of prices, for five years previous to' the time of valuation.

In 1830 famine and riot held hideous carnival. We learn from the speech from the throne that the King was determined to crush out sedition and disaffection by all the means which the law and the constitution placed at his disposal, but had no remedy to suggest for the poverty and distress of the disaffected people. In February, 1831, Mr. Smith O'Brien asked leave to bring in a Bill for the relief of the poor, but got no hope or encouragement from the Government. At this time Mr. Hume attacked the Ministry for introducing a coercive Irish policy, which was in direct opposition to the promises of conciliation they had made while they were in opposition. On the 30th March, 1831, Lord Althorpe proposed a vote of £50,000 to be advanced to commissioners for expenditure on public works in Ireland; but its effect was counterbalanced four months later by the introduction of Mr. Stanley's Arms Bill, which Lord Althorpe himself described as one of the most tyrannical measures he ever heard proposed. A Sub-letting Act, which was now under discussion, prohibited the letting of property by a lessee, unless with the express consent of the proprietor. According to Dr. Boyle, who attacked the Bill, so long as the rural population had no better employment or sure chance of subsistence than the possession of a potato field, it was idle to expect them to submit to eviction from their miserable holdings. By this time the condition of Ireland was truly desperate. Catholic Emancipation had indeed allowed Irish Catholic Members to sit in the House of Commons, but it disfranchised the forty shilling freeholders, and it gave the landlords greater opportunity for clearance.

Government answered the discontent in 1831 by another Coercion Bill. In 1834 Mr. Poulett Scrope made an unsuccessful effort to do something for the Irish tenant. In 1835 Mr. Sharman Crawford, then member for Dundalk, moved for leave to bring in a Bill to amend the law of landlord and tenant, and he reintroduced his measure on the 10th March, 1836; he obtained leave to bring in a Bill, and that was the end of it. In 1837 Mr. Lynch asked leave to bring in a Bill on waste lands, and was as unsuccessful as Mr. Sharman Crawford.

In 1842 the Irish Artificial Drainage Act did something towards the reclamation of waste lands, which, however, was of little use until amended by the Summary Proceedings Act of 1843. 1843 is a memorable epoch in the history of the Irish land agitation. It was the year of the Devon Commission, which Sir Robert Peel appointed in answer to the repeated entreaties of Mr. Sharman Crawford. The evidence of the Devon Commission, in its two years' labours, showed, as all other Commissions had shown, that the condition of the Irish peasant was miserable in the extreme—that the fatal system of land tenure was the cause of the misery; and urged that the tenant should be secured fair remuneration for his outlay of capital and labour. Lord Devon was determined that, if he could help it, the Commission should not prove valueless. On the 6th May, 1845, he printed a number of petitions, urging Parliament to secure to industrious tenants the benefits of their improvements. Lord Stanley replied by introducing a Compensation for Disturbance Bill in June, but he had to abandon it in July through the opposition of the Lords, the Commons, and the Select Committee to whom it had been entrusted. Mr. Sharman Crawford then introduced the Tenant Right Bill, which he had kept back in 1843 in order to await the result of the Devon Commission. In 1846 Lord Lincoln, urged by Mr. Sharman Crawford, brought in a Compensation for Disturbance Bill, but the Ministry resigned before it came to a second reading, and so it was forgotten. On the 10th June, 1847, Mr. Sharman Crawford's Tenant Right Bill was rejected by a majority of eighty-seven. He brought it forward again in 1848, and it was defeated on the 5th April by a majority of twenty-three. In 1848 Sir William Somerville, as Irish Secretary, brought in a Bill which was practically the same as Lord Lincoln's measure of 1846. The Irish Members supported it. The report upon the Bill was not ready until too near the end of the Session to make any further progress with it, but the Government determined that Ireland should not want some legislation during the Session, and so they suspended the Habeas Corpus Act. In 1849 Mr. Horsman urged unsuccessfully the presentation of an address pointing out to Her Majesty the condition of Ireland. Early in 1850 Sir William Somerville reintroduced his Bill, which was read a second time, given a Committee, and suffered to disappear. Mr. Sharman Crawford again unsuccessfully endeavoured to push forward his Tenant Right Bill. In 1851 Sir H. W. Barron's motion for a Committee of the whole House to inquire into the state of Ireland was negatived by a majority of nine. Nothing, therefore, had been done for the Irish tenant since the report of the Devon Commission. The Encumbered Estates Act had been passed for the Irish landlord. On the 10th February, 1852, Mr. Sharman Crawford obtained leave to bring in a Bill to regulate the Ulster custom. Then the Ministry went out of office, and the Bill, on its second reading, was rejected by a majority of 110, under Lord Derby's Conservative Government. The Government showed a disposition to do something in the Irish question. Mr. Napier, the Irish Attorney-General, drafted four Bills for regulating the relations of landlord and tenant in Ireland, a Land Improvement Bill, a Landlord and Tenant Law Consolidation Bill, a Leasing Powers Bill, and a Tenant's Improvements Compensation Bill. In 1853 the Committee appointed to consider Mr. Napier's Bills and Mr. Sharman Crawford's Bill rejected the latter measure, and considerably amended, to the disadvantage of the tenant, the fourth of Mr. Napier's measures. Since Mr. Napier had introduced them the Liberal party had come into power. Mr. Napier, though in Opposition, still did all he could to assist the passing of his own measures, but his Party fought bitterly against them. In 1854 the Bills were referred to a Select Committee of the House of Lords. The Tenant's Compensation Bill was condemned, and the other Bills sent down to the House of Commons without it. In 1855 Mr. Serjeant Shee endeavoured to bring in a Bill that was practically the same as this rejected measure, and the Government took charge of it only to abandon it before the opposition of the landlords. Mr. Sharman Crawford's Tenant Bill was in consequence introduced again by Mr. George Henry Moore, the leader of the Irish Party, in 1856, but it had to be dropped in consequence of the opposition of the Government. It was again brought forward by Mr. Moore in 1857, and again withdrawn. In 1858 Mr. Serjeant Shee's Tenant Compensation Bill was reintroduced by Mr. John Francis Maguire, then leader of the Irish Party, and defeated by a majority of forty-five. The indifference of the Government at this time to the Irish question was made the more marked by the fact that the land question of Bengal had been settled in accordance with ancient principles of Indian law, which granted to the Indian subject much that was denied the Irish subject. In 1860, however, the famous Land Act was passed which proved so unsatisfactory. The framers of the Act of 1860 tried to simplify the relations of landlord and tenant by sweeping away all remains of the feudal connection, and by establishing an absolute principle of free trade and freedom of contract as opposed to tenure.

But the Act of 1860 was a failure, in so far as it was

based upon that principle of freedom of contract which is wholly unsuited to the Irish Land Question. 'The Irish circumstances and Irish ideas as to social and agricultural economy,' said John Stuart Mill, 'are the general ideas and circumstances of the human race. It is the English ideas and circumstances that are peculiar. Ireland is in the mid-stream of human existence and human feeling and opinion. It is England that is in one of the lateral channels.'

To those who ask why the tenants take the land when they cannot fulfil their contract, the answer is, They cannot help themselves in what they do. The Irish cling to their land because all their other means of livelihood have been destroyed. They make the best terms they can, which, in truth, means bowing to whatever the master of the situation imposes. The freedom of contract argument has been very fairly disposed of by asking, 'Why does Parliament regulate, or fix and limit, the price which a railway company charges for a travelling ticket? Why are not the contracting parties, the railway company and the traveller, left to settle between them how much the price in every particular case shall be?' It is because the law says they are not free contracting parties; the railway company has a monopoly of that which is in a sense a necessity to the traveller and others. Also, if the matter were left to contract, travellers would practically have to give five shillings a mile if the company demanded it. The immediate effect of the Act was to produce an immense flood of emigration, and to create the Fenian Conspiracy. Mr. Chichester Fortescue's Bill of 1866, to amend that of 1860, of course fell through. In 1867 the Tories brought in a fresh Bill, which was practically Lord Stanley's Bill of 1845, which had to be abandoned. In 1869 Mr. Gladstone came in, and on the 15th of February, 1870, he brought in his famous Bill to Amend the Law of Landlord and Tenant in Ireland, the first Bill that really did anything to carry out the recommendation of the Devon Commission. But it did not really place the tenant beyond the vicious control of the landlord. It allowed him the privilege of going to law with the landlord; and going to law in such a case generally meant the success of the man who was longest able to fight it out. The three objects of the Land Act of 1870 were first to obtain for the tenants in Ireland security of tenure; second, to encourage the making of improvements throughout the country, and third, to get a peasant proprietorship in Ireland. It made no alteration in the tenancies held under the Ulster tenant right custom, which it merely sanctioned and enforced against the landlords of estates subject to it. The Ulster custom consists of two chief features— permissive fixity of tenure, and the tenant's right to sell the goodwill of his farm. For a long time the hope of getting the Ulster custom transferred to the other provinces was almost the highest ambition of the Irish peasant.

The framers of the Act of 1870 dared not state openly, and it was constantly denied, that the object of the new measure was to give the tenant any estate in the land, or to transfer to him any portion of the absolute ownership. Its principle of arrangement between landlord and tenant was described as a process by which bad landlords were obliged to act as the good landlords did; but it might have been more justly styled an enactment by which the amusement of evicting tenants was made a monopoly of the wealthier proprietors. The principle of compensation for disturbance which it introduced was clumsy and imperfect, and the eight clauses which attempted to create a peasant proprietorship in Ireland were no more successful than the rest of the Bill. 'The cause of their failure is obvious,' says Mr. Richey, 'to anyone acquainted with the nature of the landed estates title which it was considered desirable for the tenant to obtain. A Landed Estates Court conveyance affects not only the rights of the parties to the proceedings, but binds persons, whether parties or not, and extinguishes all rights which are inconsistent with the terms of the grant by the Court. If by any mistake more lands than should properly be sold are included in the grant, or the most indisputable rights of third parties are not noticed in the body of the grant or the annexed schedule, irreparable injustice is done and the injured parties have no redress.' The fact that the Court was not made the instrument for the perpetuation of the grossest frauds is due solely to the stringency of its rules and the intelligence of its officers.

Interwoven with all these abortive land schemes and land measures was incessant uninterrupted coercive legislation. From 1796 to 1802 an Insurrection Act was in force, and from 1797 to 1802 the Habeas Corpus Act was suspended. From 1803 to 1805 the country was under martial law, and from the same year to 1806 Habeas Corpus was suspended. Insurrection Acts were in force from 1807 to 1810, from 1814 to 1818, from 1822 to 1825. Habeas Corpus was again suspended in 1822 to 1823. In 1829, in the debate on Catholic Emancipation, Sir Robert Peel was able to say that 'for scarcely a year during the period that has elapsed since the Union has Ireland been governed by the ordinary course of law.' From the date of that utterance to the present day the country has not been governed by the ordinary law for scarcely a single year. Arms Acts, suspensions of Habeas Corpus, changes of venue, Peace Preservation Acts, and coercive measures of all kinds, succeed, accompany, and overlap each other with melancholy persistence. Roughly speaking, Ireland from the Union to 1880 was never governed by the ordinary law. The Union, according to its advocates, was to be the bond of lasting peace and affection between the two countries; it was followed by eighty years of coercive legislation. It was grimly fitting that the Union so unlawfully accomplished could only be sustained by the complete abandonment of all ordinary processes of law thereafter.

CHAPTER XI.

HOME RULE—THE LAND LEAGUE.

For some years after the failure of the Fenian insurrection there was no political agitation in Ireland; but in 1873 a new national movement began to make itself felt; this was the Home Rule Movement. It had been gradually formed since 1870 by one or two leading Irishmen, who thought the time was ripe for a new constitutional effort; chief among them was Mr. Isaac Butt, a Protestant, an eminent lawyer, and an earnest politician. The movement spread rapidly, and took a firm hold of the popular mind. After the General Election of 1874, some sixty Irish Members were returned who had stood before their constituencies as Home Rulers. The Home Rule demand is clear and simple enough; it asks for Ireland a separate Government, still allied with the Imperial Government, on the principles which regulate the alliance between the United States of America. The proposed Irish Parliament in College Green would bear just the same relation to the Parliament at Westminster that the Legislature and Senate of every American State bear to the head authority of the Congress in the Capitol at Washington. All that relates to local business it was proposed to delegate to the Irish Assembly; all questions of imperial policy were still to be left to the Imperial Government. There was nothing very startling, very daringly innovating, in the scheme. In most of the dependencies of Great Britain, Home Rule systems of some kind were already established. In Canada, in the Australasian Colonies, the principle might be seen at work upon a large scale; upon a small scale it was to be studied nearer home in the neighbouring Island of Man. One of the chief objections raised to the new proposal by those who thought it really worth while to raise any objections at all, was that it would be practically impossible to decide the border line between local affairs and imperial affairs. The answer to this is, of course, that what has not been found impossible, or indeed exceedingly difficult, in the case of the American Republic and its component States, or in the case of England and her American and Australasian Colonies, need not be found to present unsurpassable difficulties in the case of Great Britain and Ireland.

'If the Home Rule theory,' says Mr. Lecky, ' brings with it much embarrassment to English statesmen, it is at least a theory which is within the limits of the constitution, which is supported by means that are perfectly loyal and legitimate, and which, like every other theory, must be discussed and judged upon its merits.' This is exactly what English statesmen and politicians generally have refused to do. They will have none of the Home Rule theory; they will not admit that it comes within the limits of a constitutional question; Home Rule never could and never shall be granted, and so what is the use of discussing it? This was certainly the temper in which Home Rule was at first received in and out of Parliament. Of late days, politicians who have come to concede the possibility, if not the practicability of some system of local Government for Ireland, still fight off the consideration of the question by saying, 'What is the use of discussing Home Rule until you who support it present us with a clear and defined plan for our consideration?' This form of argument is no less unreasonable than the other. The supporters of Home Rule very fairly say, 'We maintain the necessity for establishing a system of local Government in Ireland. That cannot be done without the Government; till, therefore, the Government is willing to admit that Home Rule is a question to be entertained at all, it is no use bringing forward any particular plan; when it is once admitted that some system of Home Rule must be established in Ireland, then will be the time for bringing forward legislative schemes and plans, and out of the multiplicity of ideas and suggestions, creating a complete and cohesive whole.' The principle of Home Rule obtains in every State of the American Union, though the plan of Home Rule in each particular State is widely different. The principle of Home Rule obtains in every great Colony of the Crown, but the plan pursued by each Colony is of a very different kind. When the people of the two countries have agreed together to allow Ireland to manage for herself her own local affairs, it will be very easy to bring forward some scheme exactly deciding the form which the conceded Home Rule is to take. But to bring forward the completed scheme before a common basis of negotiation has been established, would be more the duty of a new Abbé Sieyès, with a new 'theory of irregular verbs,' than of a practical and serious politician.

At first the Home Rule Party was not very active. Mr. Butt used to have a regular Home Rule debate once every Session, when he and his followers stated their views, and a division was taken and the Home Rulers were of course defeated. Yet, while the English House of Commons was thus steadily rejecting year after year the demand made for Home Rule by the large majority of the Irish Members, it was affording a strong argument in favour of some system of local Government, by consistently outvoting every proposition brought forward by the bulk of the Irish Members relating to Irish Questions. In 1874 it threw out the Irish Municipal Franchise Bill, the Irish Municipal Privileges Bill, and the Bill for the purchase of Irish railways. In 1875 it threw out the motion for inquiry into the working of the Land Act, the Grand Jury Reform Bill, the Irish Municipal Corporations Bill, the Municipal Franchise Bill. In 1876 it threw out the Irish Fisheries Bill, the Irish Borough Franchise Bill, the Irish Registration of Voters Bill, and the Irish Land Bill. These were all measures purely relating to Irish affairs, which, had they been left to the decision of the Irish Members alone, would have been carried by overwhelming majorities. The Irish vote in favour of these measures was seldom less than twice as great as the opposing votes; in some cases they were three times as great, in some cases they were four, seven, and eight times greater.

Mr. Butt and his followers had proved the force of the desire for some sort of National Government in Ireland, but the strength of the movement they had created now called for stronger leaders. A new man was coming into Irish political life who was destined to be the most remarkable Irish leader since O'Connell.

Mr. Charles Stuart Parnell, who entered the House of Commons in 1875 as Member for Meath, was a descendant of the English poet Parnell, and of the two Parnells, father and son, John and Henry, who stood by Grattan to the last in the struggle against the Union. He was a grand-nephew of Sir Henry Parnell, the first Lord Congleton, the advanced Reformer and friend of Lord Grey and Lord Melbourne. He was Protestant, and a member of the Protestant Synod. Mr. Parnell set himself to form a party of Irishmen in the House of Commons who should be absolutely independent of any English political party, and who would go their own way with only the cause of Ireland to influence them. Mr. Parnell had all the qualities that go to make a good political leader, and he succeeded in his purpose. The more advanced men in and out of Parliament began to look up to him as the real representative of the popular voice. In 1878 Mr. Butt died. He had done good service in his life; he had called the Irish Home Rule Party into existence, and he had done his best to form a cohesive Parliamentary Party. If his ways were not the ways most in keeping with the political needs of the hour, he was an honest and able politician, he was a sincere Irishman, and his name deserves grateful recollection in Ireland. The leadership of the Irish Parliamentary Party was given to Mr. William Shaw, Member for Cork County, an able, intelligent man, who proved himself in many ways a good leader. In quieter times his authority might have remained unquestioned, but these were unquiet times. The decorous and demure attitude of the early Home Rule Party was to be changed into a more aggressive action, and Mr. Parnell was the champion of the change. It was soon obvious that he was the real leader recognised by the majority of the Irish Home Rule Members, and by the country behind them.

Mr. Parnell and his following have been bitterly denounced for pursuing an obstructive policy. They are often written about as if they had invented obstruction; as if obstruction of the most audacious kind had never been practised in the House of Commons before Mr. Parnell entered it. It may perhaps be admitted that the Irish Members made more use of obstruction than had been done before their time, yet it should be remembered that the early Irish obstruction was on English measures, and was carried on with the active advice and assistance of English Members. The Tory Party were then in power, and the Advanced Liberals were found often enough voting with the Obstructionists in their fiercest obstruction to the existing Government. The Irish Party fought a good fight on the famous South African Bill, a fight which not a few Englishmen now would heartily wish had proved successful. It should also be remembered that Mr. Parnell did some good service to English legislation; he worked hard to reform the Factories and Workshops Bill of 1878, the Prison Code and the Army and Navy Mutiny Bills. Many of his amendments were admitted to be of value; many in the end were accepted. His earnest efforts contributed in no small degree to the abolition of flogging in the army.

The times undoubtedly were unquiet; the policy which was called in England obstructive and in Ireland active was obviously popular with the vast majority of the Irish people. The Land Question, too, was coming up again, and in a stronger form than ever. Mr. Butt, not very long before his death, had warned the House of Commons that the old land war was going to break out anew, and he was laughed at for his vivid fancy by the English Press and by English public opinion; but he proved a true prophet. Mr. Parnell had carefully studied the condition of the Irish tenant, and he saw that the Land Act of 1870 was not the last word of legislation on his behalf. Mr. Parnell was at first an ardent advocate of what came to be known as the Three F's, fair rent, fixity of tenure, and free sale. But the Three F's were soon to be put aside in favour of more advanced ideas. Outside Parliament a strenuous and earnest man was preparing to inaugurate the greatest land agitation ever seen in Ireland. Mr. Michael Davitt was the son of an evicted tenant; his earliest youthful impressions had been of the misery of the Irish peasant and the tyranny of the Irish landlord. The evicted tenant and his family came to England, to Lancashire. The boy Michael was put to work in a mill, where he lost his right arm by a machine accident. When he grew to be a young man he joined the Fenians, and in 1870, on the evidence of an informer, he was arrested and sentenced to fifteen years' penal servitude; seven years later he was let out on ticket-of-leave. In his long imprisonment he had thought deeply upon the political and social condition of Ireland and the best means of improving it; when he came out he had abandoned his dreams of armed rebellion, and he went in for constitutional agitation to reform the Irish land system.

The land system needed reforming; the condition of the tenant was only humanly endurable in years of good harvest. The three years from 1876 to 1879 were years of successive bad harvests. The failure of the potato crop threatened the bulk of the population of Ireland with starvation. The horrors of the famine of 1847 seemed like to be seen again in Ireland. The Irish Members urged Lord Beaconsfield's Government to take some action to relieve the distress, but nothing was done and the distress increased. Early in August it was plain that the harvest was gone; the potato crop, which had fallen in 1877 from £12,400,000 to £5,200,000, had now fallen to £3,300,000; famine was close at hand. Mr. Davitt had been in America, planning out a land organization, and had returned to Ireland to carry out his plan. Land meetings were held in many parts of Ireland, and in October Mr. Parnell, Mr. Davitt, Mr. Patrick Eagan, and Mr. Thomas Brennan founded the Irish National Land League, the most powerful political organization that had been formed in Ireland since the Union. The objects of the Land League were the abolition of the existing landlord system and the introduction of peasant proprietorship.

The Land League once founded, Mr. Parnell immediately went to America to raise money to meet the distress, and while in America he was invited to state the case of Ireland before the House of Representatives at Washington. He returned to Ireland with nearly $250,000 for the relief of distress, and many thousands for the political purposes of the Land League. Relief was indeed imperative; famine was abroad, and eviction had kept pace with famine. There were over 1,200 evictions in 1876, over 1,300 in 1877, over 1,700 in 1878, and nearly 4,000 in 1879—over 10,000 evictions in four years. The Government did nothing to stay famine or eviction; it contented itself with putting Mr. Davitt and some other Land Leaguers on trial for some speeches they had made, but the prosecutions had to be abandoned. The Land League Fund, large as it was, was not nearly enough to cope with the existing distress, and fresh funds were raised by the Lord Mayor of Dublin, Mr. E. D. Gray, M.P., and by the Duchess of Marlborough, wife of the Lord-Lieutenant, whose generous action was in curious contradiction to the repeated assurances of the Government that no serious distress existed. The condition of the country was strengthening the Land League and weakening the Government. Lord Beaconsfield appealed to the country, denouncing the Liberal Party for their sympathy with Irish faction. The Home Rule Members of the House of Commons issued a manifesto calling upon Irishmen everywhere to vote against the supporters of Lord Beaconsfield's Government. The advice was implicitly followed. The General Election returned Mr. Gladstone to power at the head of a large majority. The Home Rule Party in the House was largely reinforced, chiefly by men returned under the influence of Mr. Parnell, who was now definitely elected as the leader of the Irish Parliamentary Party.

Mr. Shaw and a few friends separated themselves from Mr. Parnell's party and sat on the Ministerial side of the House, while Mr. Parnell and his followers sat with the Opposition. The Irish Party had great hopes from Mr. Gladstone's Government, on account of the strong Radical element in its constitution, and because it expressed the intention of dispensing with exceptional legislation. The Government on its part undoubtedly expected cordial allies in the members of the advanced Irish Party. Both sides were disappointed. Truly says Mr. Sullivan, 'When one looks back on the warm sympathies and the bright hopes of that hour, the realities of the situation in 1882 seem like the impossible sorrows and disappointments and disasters of a horrid dream.' It was perhaps impossible that it should be otherwise. In the excitement of a great General Election, the sympathies between the English Liberals and the Irish people were perhaps unconsciously exaggerated, and pledges were, if not made, suggested, by men striving to overthrow the Tory Government, which were not found easy to immediately satisfy when they became in their turn the members and supporters of a Government. The Irish Party, on the other hand, found that the hopes that they had entertained of speedy settlement of some of the most pressing Irish grievances were not to be realized as rapidly as they had expected. There was thus a coolness between the Government and the new Irish Party as soon as the new Parliament began, and this coolness gradually deepened into distinct hostility.

There was soon an open breach. The wretched condition of the Irish tenants, and the terrible number of evictions, led the Irish Party to bring forward a Bill for the purpose of staying evictions. The Government, who up to that time had not seen their way to take any action, then adopted some Irish suggestions in their Compensation for Disturbance Bill, which proposed to extend for a very few months a portion of the Ulster tenant right custom, which gives a dispossessed tenant compensation for improvements he may have made. It was rejected by the House of Lords, and the Government refused to take any steps to force the Lords to accept it. But they promised to bring in a comprehensive measure the next Session, and they appointed a Commission to inquire into the condition of the agricultural population of Ireland, on which Commission they absolutely refused to give any place to any representative of the tenant farmers' cause. The agitation out of doors increased. The Land League advised the people to co-operate for their own interests, and to form a sort of trade union of the tenant class, and to stand by each other in passively resisting, not merely evictions, but exactions of what they considered an unjust amount of rent above the rate of Griffith's valuation.

Griffith's valuation was undoubtedly a very rough-and-tumble way of estimating the value of land, but at least it was very much more reasonable to go by than the rates of the rack-rents. All rents therefore above Griffith's valuation were condemned by the Land League, and a practical strike was organized against the landlords extorting them. The strike was supported by a form of action, or rather inaction, which soon became historical. Boycotting, so called from the name of its first victim, meant the social excommunication of any rack-renting or evicting landlord, any oppressive agent, any land-grabber. No one who held the cause of the League dear was to work for, buy from, sell to, or hold any communication with the obnoxious persons. The process was strictly legal; nothing was to be done to the offender; nothing was to be done for him. So long as the League and its followers acted strictly within the law, kept simply on the defensive, and avoided all aggression, its position was invulnerable. The responsible leaders of the Land League always strongly condemned any other than a constitutional agitation. Mr. Michael Davitt earnestly and incessantly denounced all intimidation, all violence. In a speech on the 25th of January, 1881, he said, 'Our League does not desire to intimidate anyone who disagrees with us. While we abuse coercion we must not be guilty of coercion.' At public meetings in the county Kerry, in the same month, he called upon his hearers to 'abstain from all acts of violence,' and to 'adhere to the programme of the League, and repel every incentive to outrage.' In a speech at Tipperary he told his hearers not to allow themselves 'to be forced into the commission of any crime or any offence which will bring a stain on the national character.'

Unfortunately these counsels were not always obeyed. The famine and the accompanying evictions had left bitter fruit. Men who had been starving, who had seen their family, their friends, dying of hunger, who had been evicted to rot on the roadside for all that their landlord cared—such men were not in the spirit for wise counsels. The proud patience which the gods are said to love is not always easy to assume, at least for ignorant peasants, starving, homeless, smarting under a burning sense of wrong and a wild helpless desire for revenge. There were many outrages in different parts of the country, as there had been after every Irish famine; men were killed here and there; cattle, too, were killed and mutilated. These outrages were made the most of in England. Scattered murders were spoken of as part of a widely planned organization of massacre. People were eloquent in their sympathy for the sufferings of cattle and horses in Ireland, who never were known to feel one throb of pity at the fashionable sin of torturing pigeons at Hurlingham. But Ireland was disturbed, and for the disturbance there was what Mr. Bright had called at an earlier period of his career the ever poisonous remedy of coercion. Ministerialists argued that within ten months the mutilation of animals in Ireland had increased to forty-seven, therefore the liberties of a nation of five millions should be suspended. They forgot that in the same ten months of the same year there was a total of 3,489 convictions in England for cruelty to animals, many of the most horrible kind.

Among the Land League followers there were many Nationalists and Fenians, and there were many wild speeches made, for all of which the Government resolved to hold the leaders of the movement responsible. Mr. Parnell, Mr. Dillon, Mr. Sexton, and other Members of Parliament, were prosecuted. At the trial, Mr.

Justice Fitzgerald declared that the Land League was an illegal body. The Government cannot then have agreed with Judge Fitzgerald, or they would scarcely have allowed the League to increase in strength for the greater part of a year with impunity. The State trials came on at the close of 1880. As the jury could not agree, Mr. Parnell came back to Parliament with greater power than he ever had before. When Parliament met in 1881, it was known that Mr. Gladstone was going to bring in a Land Bill and a Coercion Bill. The Land League's advocacy of open agitation had done much to decrease the secret conspiracy and midnight outrage which Coercion Bills have always engendered. The Government refused any concession. They would not even bring in the Land Bill first, and the Coercion Bill afterwards. Then the Irish members broke away from the Government altogether, and opposed the Coercion Bill with all the means in their power that Parliamentary forms allowed. For many days they successfully impeded the measure, and the obstruction was only brought to a close in the end of February by a *coup d'état*, when the Speaker, intervening, declared that the debate must go no further. The next day Mr. Michael Davitt was arrested. The news was received with exultation in the House, and with indignation by the Irish Members, who strove to speak against it, and thirty-six were expelled from the sitting in consequence.

The severance of the extreme Irish party and the Government was now complete. Mr. Bright, who had often supported Ireland before, and was looked upon as a true friend by the Irish people, was now one of the bitterest opponents of the whole national movement and of its Parliamentary leaders. The Irish national Press was fiercely exasperated to find Mr. Bright voting for coercion for Ireland. He had indeed voted for coercion before in his younger days, but he had always been eloquent against it, and his utterances were brought up against him by the Irish papers. They reminded him that in 1866 he had described coercion for Ireland as an 'ever-failing and ever-poisonous remedy,' and they asked him why he recommended the unsuccessful and venomous legislation now. They pointed to his speech of 1849, in which he said, 'The treatment of this Irish malady remains ever the same. We have nothing for it still but force and alms.' They quoted from his speech of 1847: 'I am thoroughly convinced that everything the Government or Parliament can do for Ireland will be unavailing unless the foundation of the work be laid deep and well, by clearing away the fetters under which land is now held, so that it may become the possession of real owners, and be made instrumental to the employment and sustentation of the people. Hon. gentlemen opposite may fancy themselves interested in maintaining the present system; but there is surely no interest they can have in it which will weigh against the safety and prosperity of Ireland.' Such a passage as this might have served, it was urged, as a motto for the Land League itself. What other doctrine did the Land League uphold but that the land should become the possession of real owners, and be made instrumental to the employment and sustentation of the people? Might not the Land League have fairly asked the Government what interest it could have in the present system of land which would weigh against the safety and prosperity of Ireland? Had he not told them, too, in 1866 that 'The great evil of Ireland is this: that the Irish people—the Irish nation—are dispossessed of the soil, and what we ought to do is to provide for and aid in their restoration to it by all measures of justice.' He disliked the action of the Irish Members now, because they were acting against the Liberal Party, but had he not said in 1866 also, 'If Irishmen were united, if you 105 Members were for the most part agreed, you might do almost anything that you liked;' and further said, 'If there were 100 more Members, the representatives of large and free constituencies, then your cry would be heard, and the people would give you that justice which a class has so long denied you'? 'Exactly,' replied his Irish critics. 'We have now a united body of Irishmen, the largest and most united the House has ever seen, and you do not seem to look kindly upon it. You do not seem to be acting up to your promise made in Dublin in 1866.' 'If I have in past times felt an unquenchable sympathy with the sufferings of your people, you may rely upon it that if there be an Irish Member to speak for Ireland, he will find me heartily by his side.' At the same speech in Dublin, Mr. Bright said, 'If I could be in all other things the same, but in birth an Irishman, there is not a town in this island I would not visit for the purpose of discussing the great Irish question, and of rousing my countrymen to some great and united action.' 'This is exactly what we are doing,' said his Land League critics; 'why do you denounce us now? Why do you vote for Coercion Acts to prevent the discussion of the great Irish question?'

But all such recriminations were vain and valueless. Mr. Bright had changed his opinions, and there was no more use in reminding him that he had once encouraged Irish agitation than in taunting Mr. Gladstone with having been once a member of the Tory Party. That Mr. Bright was no longer a friend to the leaders of Irish public opinion, that he was no longer at the side of those who undoubtedly represented the feeling of the nation, was a matter indeed for regret. A friend the less, an enemy the more, is always to be regretted. But they had to go on and do the best they could without him; they could not turn from the course of their duty, even because a great speaker and a great statesman did not think and act in his old age as he had thought and acted when he was younger.

After the Coercion Act was passed, one or two men were arrested, and then the Government arrested Mr. John Dillon. Mr. John Dillon was one of the most extreme of the Irish Members. His father was Mr. John B. Dillon, the rebel of 1848, and one of the founders of the *Nation* newspaper. When the rebellion was crushed, John Dillon escaped to France, and returned to England years later, under the general amnesty, and was elected for the County Tipperary. He earned honourable distinction in the House of Commons by his efforts to bring about an alliance between the Irish Party and the English Radicals, and some of Mr. John Bright's speeches contain the warmest tributes to his honour and his ability. Mr. John Dillon, the son, was a man of much more extreme opinions. He was imbued with the intense detestation of English rule which English politicians find it difficult to understand, and he never seemed to have much sympathy with or belief in Parliamentary agitation. Some months after his imprisonment Mr. Dillon was released, on account of ill health. The Coercion Bill proved a hopeless failure. The Government did their best by imprisoning members of the Land League, local leaders, priests, and others, in all directions, to give the country over again into the hands of Ribbonmen and other conspirators, and take it out of the hands of the constitutional agitators. The Land Bill was passed, and proved to be utterly inadequate to the purpose it was intended to serve.

With the conclusion of Parliament a Land League Convention was summoned in the Rotunda, Dublin, in the early days of September, 1881. The Convention represented the public feeling of Ireland, as far as public opinion ever can be represented by a delegated body. The descendants of the Cromwellian settlers of the north sat side by side with men of the rebel blood of Tipperary, with the impetuous people of the south, with the strong men of the midland hunting counties. The most remarkable feature of the meeting was the vast number of priests who were present.

The attitude of the Catholic clergy of Ireland towards the League was very remarkable. It was said at first, by those who did not understand the Irish clergy, that the Church and the League would never form an alliance. The Land League soon began to gain powerful supporters among the Irish ecclesiastics. Archbishop MacCabe had attacked it early in the movement. His attack had raised up a powerful champion of the Land League in Archbishop Croke, of Cashel. The Nationalists welcomed Archbishop Croke as their religious leader, and he travelled through Ireland in a sort of triumph, receiving from the pesantry everywhere the most enthusiastic reception. The priests in general began to accept the Land League programme enthusiastically. The priesthood have always been the warmest supporters of any movement that has really appeared to promise to do good to the Irish people. Clerical sympathy with the Land League was in itself a proof of its law-abiding and constitutional principles, which ought to have counted for much with the Government. But the Government appeared to be obstinately shut against all impressions. Instead of being impressed by the significance of the ecclesiastical support of the League, the Government seemed determined to force the priests and the Leaguers into closer sympathy by arresting, on the 20th of May, a Catholic priest, Father Eugene Sheehy, of Kilmallock. A great number of priests spoke at the Convention, young and old; all were in warm sympathy with the League and its leaders. The meeting was singularly quiet; the speeches were moderate in the extreme; but the country was in a terribly disordered state, and even the strong force of coercion struggled in vain against the general disorganization.

At this crisis the Government, for some reason or other, liberated Father Sheehy, who at once commenced a vigorous crusade against the Ministry, and his entry into Cork, in company with Mr. Parnell, resembled a Roman triumph. The Government was now determined to make a bold stroke. Mr. Gladstone made a bitter attack on Mr. Parnell, to which Mr. Parnell fiercely replied, and a few days after a descent was made upon the leaders of the Land League. Mr. Parnell, Mr. Sexton, Mr. Dillon, and the chief officers of the League were arrested, and conveyed to Kilmainham prison. Mr. Egan, who was in Paris, and some others, escaped arrest. An address was at once issued to the Irish tenants, signed by the imprisoned Land Leaguers, and calling upon them to pay no rent until their leaders were liberated. The Government immediately declared the Land League illegal, and suppressed its branches throughout the country. The result was a great increase in the outrages, and the country became more disturbed than ever. The men who could have kept it quiet, who had restrained the popular feeling, were in prison, and the secret societies had it all their own way. This period was disgraced by several murders—the murder of two bailiffs, the Huddys, in Connemara; the murder of an informer in Dublin; of Mrs. Smythe, and Mr. Herbert.

After a while Mr. Sexton was liberated on account of ill-health, and the imprisonment of the other Land League leaders was evidently a great embarrassment to the Government. Private overtures of freedom were made to them, if they would consent to leave the country for a time—at least of freedom, if they would consent to cross the Channel to the Continent, even though they came back the next day. But the prisoners refused any such compromise. They considered that they had been unfairly imprisoned, and they would accept no conditions. Meanwhile the affairs of the country were going from bad to worse. The Government were unable to cope with the disaffection, and the Land Act was unavailing to meet the misery of the people. What Mr. Parnell has always predicted has come to pass. The Land Courts were overcrowded with work; there were thousands of cases in hand which it would take years to dispose of, and in the meantime the people were suffering terribly, and the landlords were taking every advantage of the delay. To meet the difficulty, Mr. Parnell sent out from his prison the draft of an Arrears Bill, to relieve the tenant from the pressure of past rent, and this measure was practically accepted by the Government, who promised, if the Irish Party withdrew their measure, to bring in a Ministerial Bill to the same effect. Fresh surprises were in store. Rumours of a change of policy on the part of the Government were suddenly confirmed by the liberation of Mr. Parnell, Mr. Dillon, Mr. O'Kelly, and many other of the Land League prisoners, and, more surprising still, by the release of Mr. Michael Davitt.

Ever since the suppression of the Land League the fiercer spirit of the secret societies had been abroad in Ireland. The Land League and its constitutional agitation had always been disliked by the men who formed them, and the Ministerial concessions pointed at a reconcilement which they detested.

The Ministry seemed really to have awakened to the gravity of the situation, and to have suddenly accepted Fox's theory of the necessity of governing Ireland according to Irish ideas. Mr. Forster, the most uncompromising opponent of such a theory, resigned, and Lord Frederick Cavendish, a younger son of the Duke of Devonshire, was appointed Chief Secretary for Ireland in his place. Then came the terrible tragedy which shattered the fair fortune which seemed to have come at last to Ireland. On Saturday the 6th May, 1882, Lord Frederick Cavendish landed in Dublin; that same evening he and Mr. Burke, one of the Castle officials, were murdered in the Phœnix Park in the clear summer twilight by assassins who escaped at the time. Irishmen should always remember that at a time when England and all the world were thrilled with horror at the murder, at a time when the passions of men might well be stirred to their worst, the tone of English opinion and of the English Press, with rare exceptions, was just and temperate. The Irish leaders, Mr. Parnell, Mr. Davitt, and Mr. Dillon, issued a manifesto to the Irish people, expressing in their own heart-stricken grief the sorrow and the shame of the Party and the people they represented. The document concluded, 'We feel that no act has been perpetrated in our country during the exciting struggles for social and political rights of the past fifty years that has so stained the name of hospitable Ireland as this cowardly and unprovoked assassination of a friendly stranger, and that until the murderers of Lord Frederick Cavendish and Mr. Burke are brought to justice, that stain will sully our country's name.' At meetings all over the country the crime was no less bitterly denounced, and the Corporation of Dublin passed a resolution declaring that until the perpetrators of the crime were brought to justice all Irishmen must feel dishonoured.

The Government at once brought in a Crimes Bill, one of the most stringent ever passed against Ireland. They then brought in, and carried, after strong opposition in the House of Lords, the Arrears Bill, a measure to enable the tenant-farmers of Ireland, under certain conditions, to wipe out the arrears of rent which had accumulated upon them.

In the August of 1882 a National Exhibition of Irish manufactures was opened in Dublin, the first enterprise of the kind ever conducted by the National Party, in complete independence from Castle patronage; it was a great success. On the day that the exhibition was opened, a statue of O'Connell was unveiled in Sackville Street, opposite the O'Connell Bridge, and a vast procession of all the guilds and associations of Dublin was organized in its honour. There was a conviction in England, and in the minds of the Castle authorities, that such an event could not pass off without some desperate scenes of disorder, if not of insurrection. But the peace and order of Ireland's capital city was not disturbed, and the spectacle of the vast procession, many miles in length, of the stately statue that had been raised to a national hero, of the beautiful building richly stored with the work of Irish hands and the creations of Irish intellect, all accomplished entirely by the Irish people themselves, under the guidance of their national leaders, without foreign aid or countenance, afforded one of the strongest arguments in favour of Home Rule ever advanced in Ireland. A people who could carry out so successfully, with such perfect peace and order, so difficult an enterprise, might be admitted, even by the most prejudiced, to have within them all the capacity for successful self-government.

On the day following the O'Connell Centennial, the freedom of the City of Dublin was conferred on Mr. Parnell and Mr. Dillon. The same day another popular Irish member, Mr. E. D. Gray, M.P., was committed to Richmond Prison, O'Connell's old prison, on a charge of contempt of court, which was the cause of a Parliamentary inquiry into the exercise of that curious judicial privilege. Mr. Gray was the owner of the *Freeman's Journal*, and at the time was High Sheriff of Dublin. He had written in his paper some censures on the conduct of a jury whose verdict had sentenced a man to death. The judge before whom the case had been tried, Mr. Justice Lawson, immediately sent Mr. Gray to prison for three months for contempt of court and fined him £500. After two months' imprisonment Mr. Gray was released; the fine was paid by subscription in a few days. When Parliament met in a winter Session, the case was brought forward as one of privilege and submitted to a Select Committee.

At one time during the autumn of 1882, the Irish Executive seemed likely to be much embarrassed by a strike among the Irish Constabulary, a body of men on whom the Executive naturally were forced to depend greatly. Some hundreds of police struck; there were some fierce disturbances in Dublin—at one time it seemed as if the police in every town in Ireland were discontented and prepared to combine against the Government; but the Government made some concessions, and what at one time seemed a very serious danger faded away into nothingness.

In October another National Convention was held in Dublin, and a new and vast organization formed, embracing in one all the Irish demands for Home Rule and for Land Reform. With its inauguration begins a new chapter in Irish history.

THE END.

www.ingramcontent.com/pod-product-compliance
Lightning Source LLC
Chambersburg PA
CBHW021917180426
43199CB00032B/433